PENGUIN BOOKS

MAKEOVERS FROM THE BUDGET GARDENER

Maureen Gilmer is the author of nine books on gardening, including *The Budget Gardener* (also available from Penguin), and her articles and photographs have appeared in national magazines, including *Better Homes & Gardens* and *Country Living*. She is an award-winning professional landscape designer and consultant for commercial and residential projects. Her full-color Internet Web site, *The Landscape-Garden Forum*, has received a Magellan award for excellence and may be found at http://www.gardenforum.com. She has appeared numerous times on national television, including on the Discovery Channel program *Home Matters*, and *Willard Scott's Home & Garden Almanac*, which airs on the Home & Garden Television Network. She lives in Dobbins, California.

MAKEOVERS FROM THE BUDGET GARDENER

TRANSFORMING YOUR GARDEN IN JUST ONE SEASON

MAUREEN GILMER

PENGUIN BOOKS

PENGUIN BOOKS

Published by the Penguin Group

Penguin Books USA Inc., 375 Hudson Street, New York, New York 10014, U.S.A.
Penguin Books Ltd, 27 Wrights Lane, London W8 5TZ, England
Penguin Books Australia Ltd, Ringwood, Victoria, Australia
Penguin Books Canada Ltd, 10 Alcorn Avenue, Toronto, Ontario, Canada M4V 3B2
Penguin Books (N.Z.) Ltd, 182–190 Wairau Road, Auckland 10, New Zealand

Penguin Books Ltd, Registered Offices: Harmondsworth, Middlesex, England

First published in Penguin Books 1997

1 3 5 7 9 10 8 6 4 2

Copyright © Maureen Gilmer, 1997
All rights reserved

Illustrations by the author

"Tulip Planting Guide" appearing on page 114 is reproduced by permission of the Netherlands
Flower Bulb Information Center.

LIBRARY OF CONGRESS CATALOGING IN PUBLICATION DATA
Gilmer, Maureen.
Makeovers from the budget gardener: transforming your garden in just one season / Maureen Gilmer.
p.   cm.
Includes bibliographical references and index.
ISBN 0 14 02.6003 X (pbk.)
1. Landscape gardening.   I. Title.
SB473.G552   1997
712'.6—dc20   96–45971

Printed in the United States of America
Set in Usherwood Book
Designed by Michael Mendelsohn of MM Design 2000, Inc.

To my husband, Jim,
the great man
who stands quietly
behind the woman

A penny saved is a penny earned.

ACKNOWLEDGMENTS

 Many thanks to the many women who support me: to Susan Urstadt, who never gave up on the budget-gardening idea; to Jeanne Fredericks, who made it a reality; and to my editor, Jane von Mehren, who diligently saw this book through to completion.

PREFACE

*The difference between good architecture and bad architecture
is ten years' growth of vines.*
Wisdom of the Budget Gardener

 The two words that best describe the focus of this book are: *fast* and *cheap*. Fast because you want to leap into gardening and make your outdoor surroundings beautiful right now, and cheap because you have only a small amount of money to spend.

Giving your landscape a fast and cheap makeover is similar to redecorating the interior of your home with discount paint, wallpaper, window coverings, and carpeting. A good interior decorator can work miracles with a timeworn living room or kitchen if she knows the tricks of the trade. A landscape designer can completely change the character of a garden just as quickly using seasonal bedding plants, some wood stain, and paving units. You can achieve the very same thing with a little guidance and a reliable palette of quick-to-bloom plants.

Your home is your sanctuary, a comforting cocoon separated from a congested world. These days, many people are gaining a new appreciation of just how beautiful and safe their old backyard can be. In fact, spending time to redo and replant cheaply may mean entertaining at home more often, which saves money on everything from gas to parking to restaurants. And there is no reason why anyone should not begin this process since all it entails is a few dollars to spend on seeds and pots.

The act of gardening itself is an age-old therapy loved by civilizations both rich and poor, with each seed a heavenly gift and every plant a living promise of beauty. Why not rekindle your vital link with the Earth by giving your tired homesite a creative garden makeover? By the end of this year, or even this very season, your efforts will be rewarded with beauty, color, and a lasting sense of personal satisfaction for many years to come.

HOW TO USE THIS BOOK

While you can build the exact same house on almost any lot, every garden, like a person's fingerprints, will always be different from another. This is because a garden must respond to your personal needs and the environmental conditions specific to a site, such as soils, local climate, and topography. That's why the focus of this book is on the process of redecorating the landscape, because predesigned plans are neither effective nor affordable.

There are many reasons for redecorating your landscape, and everyone has a different image in mind. Perhaps you've become intrigued by gardening as a hobby or just want a beautiful and relaxing outdoor space. If you're an aficionado of *nouvelle cuisine,* then your reasons may be motivated by the lure of fresh baby lettuce and spicy chives among the flower beds. Or perhaps you are about to host a large event such as a wedding or reception in your garden.

This book is for everyone who wants to garden, even if you have only a fire escape, balcony, townhouse yard, or condo courtyard. It is your road map to redoing your yard on a budget and achieving the boldest impact. It begins by helping you understand the assets and liabilities of your garden, then details how the local growing season influences both what and when you plant.

To start with, you will learn about the shoestring plant palette, a veritable treasure trove of fast-growing flowers such as petunias, pansies, and zinnias that landscapers know are reliable performers. All are so easy to grow even a rank beginner is assured success the very first year, and some, like sweet pea and morning glory, cost just pennies per plant when the seed is sown directly into garden soil. Among these pages you'll find a process for designing with these plants that's as easy as using a coloring book, followed by a surefire method of accurately estimating your costs ahead of time. You will also find quick and easy restoration ideas for all your "hardscape"—the constructed elements from fences to shade arbors—as well as suggestions for the creation of ingenious illusions. For every penny you save on restoring what you have and purchasing only the essential materials and equipment, you'll have that much more to spend on beautiful flowering plants.

To make the most of this book, read and use *The Budget Gardener* to discover more cheap or free alternatives to expensive garden products. Why live with your tired, worn-out landscape, or stare at the bare ironwork of your balcony railing, when it could be overflowing with vibrant, colorful flowers? When you're through with your budget garden makeover, the neighbors won't believe your stunning flower garden is a bare-bones budget garden.

CONTENTS

Makeovers
from the
Budget Gardener

CHAPTER 1

PLANNING YOUR PROJECT

You don't buy a garden . . . you create one.
Wisdom of the Budget Gardener

Everyone has a different image or big idea in mind for their garden. A big idea may be a design theme based on architectural style or it may relate to a design philosophy, such as "accentuate the positive and eliminate the negative," when there's no architectural style to work with. But for our purposes the big idea relates to time and money. Fast gardens and, preferably, cheap ones force you to balance cost, time, and beauty without sacrificing quality. Think hard about your own needs and decide which of these two categories best describes what you have in mind.

The Special Occasion: The instant landscapes of the rich and famous are usually created for an outdoor party or gathering. To achieve a fast transformation, the landscape must be created in a way that ensures the garden is at its color peak by a certain date. This means cleanup must come first so that plants are in the ground in time to adjust and resume blooming vigorously by the designated date.

The key to these gardens is defining the window of opportunity to achieve your goals. These time limitations will influence every decision you make from start to finish. For example, if you're planning a garden party and have just a week to spruce up the yard, then your palette of plants will be limited to high-profile annual flowers purchased in larger container sizes that assure they are already well into their blooming season. These plants cost you more because of their age, which is the price you pay for such short notice. In contrast, if it's March and you're planning for an August wedding, you have all spring and most of the summer to prepare. You'll be able to save money by growing some plants from seed, which costs just pennies. Other color bedding plants may be purchased as very small container-grown seedlings for a fraction of the cost of the older blooming ones, yet in the long run they all reach the same size at maturity. In this case it is clear that time does indeed mean money.

Another example of special-occasion planning is when you make improvements to your front and backyards before putting your house on the market. Curb appeal, a term used to describe the first impression of the front yard, is critical to how fast and well your house will sell. A healthy injection of seasonal color can make a substantial difference.

Shoestring Makeovers: If you're tired of looking at a barren yard or out-of-date or ragged landscaping but don't have much to spend, then a shoestring makeover is just what the doctor ordered. This is the outdoor version of budget decorating that gives you a program for low-cost improvement for both your constructed elements and planting. Anyone moving into a home with tired landscaping wants to jump in and make improvements right off, but moving expenses may leave very little in your pocket for the garden. Time is not nearly as important as cost, but the goal is still to achieve a brilliant color garden the very first year.

Whether you are working toward a special occasion or a makeover, design fundamentals remain the same; the only difference is the size of new plants and extent of preparation activity. There is nothing too complex for most people to accomplish because the following chapters will lay the process out in detail. You need only heed the advice and give a lot of thought to exactly what you like, so that the final product—the garden—will be best suited to your personal taste and practical needs.

HOME STYLE—GARDEN STYLE

The homes we admire on the pages of glossy magazines are beautifully decorated with designs that flow right through doors and windows to blend with the spaces outside. In these schemes you'll see that the rooms appear larger when this transition is well done because the decorator has borrowed space either physically or visually from outside. For those who live in the city, every inch of ground is precious, making the need for such a link even more important. It makes sense to treat your yard and garden with the same attention you give paint and wallpaper indoors. In fact, the way a garden is designed is very similar to the way a room is decorated.

You should consider your outside space or yard as a garden room. The walls around your outdoor rooms consist of fences, existing shrubs, and trees. There may be windows in these walls looking onto the street or into the neighbor's yard, or, best of all, they open onto a pleasant view. Your ceiling is the sky or tree canopies, while the floor coverings are typically paving or lawn. And, just as with indoor rooms, you have decorative art in the garden combined with attractive outdoor furniture arrangements. Whenever you feel overwhelmed by the task of redecorating your yard, always go back to this outdoor room concept and you'll find solutions based upon what you already know about interiors.

But there are also important differences which make outdoor redecorating a bit more complex and intimidating. First, there is the problem of time. You can paint or paper a bedroom in a weekend to completely transform its character, but even the fastest-growing annual plants require a few weeks to have a similar impact. Second is the fact that a garden is alive while a room is inanimate. Anything that is living requires some degree of nurture and attention if it is to thrive. Third is the problem of skill, because it is much simpler to roll paint over a wall than it is to choose plants, prepare soil, and plant. But despite all these differences, redecorating the yard can be one of your most satisfying home improvement projects.

Just as a fine painting is enhanced by its frame, the landscape that surrounds your house is as important to the overall quality of the homesite as your house itself. Today's most popular home styles can be grouped into distinct categories whose elements should be reflected in the garden so there is a smooth transition from building to landscape. When a home and its landscape fail to support each other the entire site is jeopardized. For example, a colonial home planted with exotic plants such as New Zealand flax or elephant ear will result in an uncomfortable mix that fails to appear integrated even to the untrained eye. Among the most traditional styles are many adaptations of colonial, American country, Mediterranean and Victorian architecture, but in many newer homes there may be characteristics of all three. The following list of major styles will help you to decide how to integrate your home and garden:

Colonial: The people of New England, where this style originated, were conservative and orderly, and their architecture reflected this as well as the austere climate. Homes were boxy, without decoration, and most often made of stone or brick combined with painted wood clapboard siding or naturally weathered shingles. Their gardens were simple, composed of square and rectangular beds that gave a rigid, semiformal appearance.

American Country: The pioneers who traveled west built their homes with the trees of the endless forests they encountered. Homesteads began with log cabins later replaced by sturdy frame houses with large porches, often painted white. This farmhouse style is such a part of our heritage that it inspired the American country decorating movement complemented by the true cottage gardens we so love. Historically these were the places where a conglomeration of plants grew—whatever could be found in the isolation of rural farm and ranch life.

Mediterranean: With its origins in Persia, the Middle East, and southern Europe, the Mediterranean style responded to the needs of those who lived in a hot, dry climate that lacked timber for construction. Homes built of packed earth were not only cooler but evolved into the Spanish and Pueblo styles that remain intensely popular even today. Among the plants in these gardens are native wildflowers, dripping colorful vines, and a profusion of foliage plants to soften the highly reflective stucco surfaces.

Victorian: In the nineteenth century, American industry created an environment where opportunity bridged the barriers between rich and poor. Those who achieved a certain degree of newfound wealth sought to display it in tasteful architecture. Elaborate detailing and gingerbread exteriors mirrored cluttered interior design, which was carried out into the garden in a collection of the rare and exotic. Classical ornament, brilliant but controlled bedding flower displays, and miniature botanical gardens became the formula for period garden design.

Keep in mind that these home garden styles are only guidelines, not hard and fast rules. Most of us live in homes built after World War II which can't be classified so easily, but don't let this discourage you, because bland architecture has no constraints. It presents a blank canvas on which to create a garden that is an outward expression of your inner self. It is a place to show your love of flowers and color and even the romance of gardens past. If you dream of a casual country garden, or one that suggests the orderly colonial style, go ahead and create one. Your only limitation is your imagination.

EVALUATING YOUR YARD

The first and perhaps the most important step in this process is to take a realistic look at your yard. It's not as easy as you think; spaces we've looked at year in and year out tend to lose their clarity. This can be likened to a child who grows up so gradually that the only time we really notice the changes is when looking at old photos for comparison. The changes are just as subtle in a yard: plants become overgrown, the lawn dies out in patches, and the fence boards bleach out and crack. Yet all of these are critical factors in overall visual quality.

To help you see the details better, consider all elements discussed here and assess whether they present assets or liabilities in your own garden. Separate the landscape into two categories: the first is the hardscape or constructed elements; the second is the status of the plants. Both are equally important no matter how large or small your yard.

THE HARDSCAPE

Hardscape is a word used by landscapers to describe all sorts of nonplant materials and structures, from small buildings to fences and paving. Hardscape is one of the most expensive parts of the garden to replace, so it is wise to preserve and improve what you have rather than replace it.

This is not that easy to do because we are saturated with magazines, books, and TV shows that demonstrate a variety of home improvement ideas, including lots of new products they would love us to buy. But the budget gardener cannot afford such luxuries. In addition, sometimes the new products are of poorer quality than our older traditional materials and tools. And despite the fact that you are taking on all the labor as a do-it-yourself project, these programs never explain how to pay the high cost of raw materials. Let's face it, if the materials are too expensive, even the most skilled gardener will never enjoy the elaborate projects we see promoted so avidly.

It might be easier for you to evaluate your hardscape by classifying everything into loose categories based on size. It is much easier to work from the ground up or from the highest point down than to approach it arbitrarily. The "ground plane" consists of wood decks, paving, and in-ground swimming pools or spas. Anything above your head should be slotted into the "overhead" category. This includes shade structures, arbors, and buildings of all kinds. In between are fences, walls, and raised planters. It's also important to know how such elements are built in order to better understand your options when repairing, replacing, or improving them.

Paving: Paving is used to create walkways, patios, pool decking, and sports courts. Paving can be made of a continuous pour such as asphalt or concrete, or of individual unit pavers.

Asphalt is the cheaper of the two continuous-pour types and is much more flexible than concrete. If there is expansion or contraction of the soil underneath, asphalt's flexible nature can move with the ground. This sometimes results in low spots or "bird baths," where the soil has contracted too much under the paving layer. Asphalt is only available in black, which has traditionally restricted its use to driveways and sports courts.

Concrete slabs are rigid and often crack due to soil heaving under extremes of weather. To accommodate this variation in the slab, contractors install expansion joints at regular intervals to take up the stress. These joints may consist of pressed felt, wood, or plastic. You may also find score joints, which are simply grooves made in the wet slab to control where the inevitable cracking occurs. Older concrete slabs not only suffer cracking, but they also become stained by oil or water spots or blackened with mildew.

Paving that consists of individual unit pavers is typically of brick, interlocking pavers, or concrete paving units. Unit pavers can be laid over a foundation slab of poured concrete and their joints filled with mortar. This is the strongest, most long-lasting of all unit paver installation methods but is also the most expensive since you cover the ground twice. A cheaper alternative is to create a foundation or setting bed of leveled and compacted sand bound by wood edging boards. The unit pavers are laid out on top of the sand, set edge-to-edge without mortar. The edging boards, usually 2-by-6-inch foundation grade redwood, are staked solidly into place and firmly hold the outside rows.

This sand-based installation causes the most problems in clay soils because these soils suffer the most extreme expansion and contraction. But since these installations do not include mortar joints, they are the simplest to repair. In fact, many European cities are using interlocking pavers on sand for their downtown streets since the utilities beneath are often very old and require frequent repair. Rather than tear up solid paving, they simply remove the pavers, make a repair, and set them back in place again.

Wood Decking: Decks are relatively new in landscaping terms and do not enjoy the same life span as standard paving. Even high-grade redwood decks suffer from loose connections and warping, plus wear and tear, which makes them unattractive after a few decades. Just like concrete, wood also expands and contracts with the weather, forcing nail heads up and out of position. Nail heads and splintering are real hazards of older decks, along with the loosening of steps and stairway connections.

Some decks at homes near the ocean are painted to protect against salt air. Others are left to weather naturally despite the salt air because the homeowner loves the aged gray patina of redwood or cedar. Elsewhere it is not uncommon to find painted decks, particularly if the wood is an inferior fir or pine that looks cleaner and lasts longer with a protective coating of paint. Problems with paint that peels or chips in damp climates or under excessive wear are normal. None of these finish preferences are wrong—they are just different.

Overheads: The most common types of overheads are shade arbors and trellises that support climbing plants. Typically constructed out of cedar or redwood, they may be painted or simply sealed to weather naturally. These structures take a real beating from the elements, but those with big posts and beams will last many decades. Lath and 2-by-2s have a tendency to warp or twist and crack over time. Old Victorian trellises are made of much smaller-size lumber which deteriorates rapidly, and thus we no longer see many of them.

Until the 1970s, many arbors and trellises were painted. Then the natural wood look emerged, making dark stains more popular than the traditional white paint. Now we have come full circle and rediscovered whitewash, with its ability to enhance the beauty of plants and manipulate light. Where dark stains absorbed what light there was under shade arbors, white paint magnifies it so that the spaces are more cheerful. White, beige, and light grays all provide a neutral, high-contrast background that makes the foliage and flowers of vines stand out. When considering a renovation job on overheads, remember this light-versus-dark-colored finish if you are looking for a more dramatic effect.

Fences: The vast majority of American backyards are enclosed by wood fences. In many landscapes, it is the single largest constructed element, and a discolored, worn, leaning, or damaged fence can have a negative impact on any home. Fortunately this is also the easiest element to repair yourself. You may also want to consider painting or staining your fence to match the house or other structures nearby for an integrated look.

Iron fencing of any kind, be it wrought, tubular, or cast, suffers rusting problems. These types of fences are usually found either in the front yard, where its decorative touch is most seen and appreciated, or around swimming pools as a protective barrier. When the bases of the iron posts sit upon paving, they eventually begin shedding rust, leaving a noticeable stain. Chain-link fence posts also can develop this rust problem, particularly in coastal areas where the salt air is devastating to all metals. Controlling rust is difficult and requires metal preparation and repainting. Remember also that if you do not prepare the metal, the paint will flake off.

Masonry Walls: Anything you build with mortar and masonry units, such as concrete block or brick, is technically masonry, but most often it refers to walls of various heights and thicknesses.

There are two basic ways that walls are built. The most common method uses a concrete block core covered by an outer veneer of brick, stone, or similar accent material. Concrete blocks have two cells in each block which provide space for reinforcing rods, or "rebar" for short. These rods are embedded in the foundation and extend to the top of the wall. The cells also add to the strength of the wall, because once it is completed, they are filled with concrete, which sets up around the rods. A good block wall is filled solid and becomes a single integrated mass.

The second method for building a masonry wall uses straight brick or stone, but the units must be very thick to achieve structural integrity since these materials lack spaces to accommodate reinforcing steel rebar. Using the block core method is preferable since it not only ensures your wall is stable, it also reduces the need for the more expensive accent materials.

Walls are usually classified as freestanding walls, seatwalls, or retaining walls. Freestanding walls, usually six feet in height, provide a long-lasting but expensive perimeter barrier. They can also act like partitions in a garden to define or separate spaces at heights varying from three to six feet. Seatwalls are low and fat so you can sit on them comfortably. Seatwalls may be part of a raised planter or simply function on their own as permanent outdoor seating. A true retaining wall is designed with an oversized underground footing to give it the strength to hold back wet soil. Smaller retaining-like walls around raised planters act more like curbs and thus lack the larger footing.

Walls that hold back soil, no matter how tall, all share the problem of discoloration. When they are built, a waterproof sealer should be applied to the back of the wall before the soil is replaced. If it was never applied, or if the wall is so old the sealer has disintegrated, moisture will enter the wall and travel through it to the outside face. In the process, lime from the concrete or mortar moves too, and accumulates on the outside of the wall in white or gray deposits.

Many walls have been constructed with a series of weep holes along the bottom to allow moisture accumulating behind the wall to drain through and out the front, reducing the tendency for water to move through the wall. The continuous draining at weep holes, however, often causes staining from algae growth in moist environments. You can clean up weep holes and loosen mineral buildup by applying muriatic acid products along the base of the wall and adjacent paving. These products are sold by most swimming pool supply stores.

Problem Areas: Every house and yard is different, but nearly every one has at least one problem area. It may be on your lot or that of a neighbor, but either way the problem should be addressed in your planning process in order to reduce its impact. If you are planning for a special event, your solution may be temporary, while a shoestring makeover should treat it in a more permanent way.

Garbage cans have to go somewhere, usually in a sideyard, but if that isn't possible they may be out in full view. The best solution is to build simple screen fence panels on one, two, or more sides—depending on what it takes to hide them. For temporary screening you can use silk or plastic ficuslike trees obtained from the party rental agency, or real greenery borrowed from the local garden center's container stock.

The same applies to electric and gas utilities, propane tank, well head, air conditioning unit, and the meters that are frequently fastened to the house. All of these may also be screened off with a panel of lattice, grape stake fencing, or other lightweight materials. Remember that the power company comes to read the meter so it must remain readily accessible.

THE LIVING SOFTSCAPE

The next stage in evaluating what you have is to study the plants that are already growing in the landscape. Keep in mind that every tree, shrub, or vine you have is important since they required many years to mature. Replacing them isn't so much a matter of money—it's a matter of time.

Trees: Older trees have a big impact on your lot. Big oppressive trees can make gardening beneath their canopies virtually impossible due to both dense shade and surface roots. We grow fond of our trees that were once small, widely spaced saplings that have grown so large there is hardly space between them. This tight spacing not only affects the health and form of the trees, it shades the entire yard so that the lawn and most other plants struggle to grow and bloom. Even though we see a lot of emphasis on planting trees to improve the environment, it's more important to ensure the trees we have remain healthy. Sometimes that means removal of an individual tree to allow those that remain to grow better. It may also mean that their canopies should be thinned to allow more sunlight to penetrate through the interior branches and into the garden below.

Your goal in planning a makeover or preparing for a party is to take advantage of the best that your trees offer and eliminate as many of the problem trees as you can. If you don't feel comfortable making the following evaluation on your own, contact a certified arborist listed in the Yellow Pages and he or she will help you with the decision. The small sum you pay for their services is worthwhile since you need not worry that you've removed a tree needlessly.

To make the right choices on your own, use a process of elimination based on the following problems that most often afflict trees in residential neighborhoods:

1. **Peeling bark:** Trees experience sunburn and insect damage on their trunks that seriously threaten their longevity and overall health. The practice of painting the trunks of orchard trees white is to reflect direct sunlight enough to prevent sunburn and blistering. Sunburn is the avenue by which borers, one of our most damaging tree pests, enter otherwise healthy trees. Younger trees that lack the canopy to shade their trunks are the most vulnerable to this. Inspect for signs of peeling bark and mealy sawdust underneath the bark that indicate borers.

    Peeling or damaged bark can also be caused by careless lawn mowing or string trimmers that gouge or tear at the bark near the base of the trunk. Any tree that has been "ring barked" cannot transport moisture and nutrients since the damage cuts off the vital tissue. If the tree is suffering from this kind of damage it may never thrive.

2. **Dripping and litter:** When trees are stressed by drought, saturated soils, or when planted in harsh climates, they become vulnerable to pests. Both scale insects and aphids exude a substance called honeydew which ants love, so you frequently find them on afflicted trees. The honeydew may appear yellow, semiclear, and sticky. It can also turn black when a common fungus mold grows on the substance. Honeydew dripping off a tree canopy can make your deck, patio furniture, automobiles, and paving sticky as well as discolored. If you have the choice of removing a dripping tree or a healthy one, always remove the dripper.

Similarly, trees that drop litter, be it fruit, leaves, seed pods, or copious flowers, present a continual maintenance problem and a real hazard to foot traffic. If the tree is beautiful and healthy, putting up with the litter is worthwhile, but if you have another tree nearby to compensate, you may want to choose to remove this litterer. Keep in mind that some trees that are seriously stressed will make a final push to reproduce by fruiting or flowering heavily.

3. **Age:** Some trees are naturally more long-lived than others. It seems that those that are fast-growing during their early years, such as poplar, willow, and alder, tend to have a shorter life span than such slower-growing species as oak. Always choose to remove the short-life trees in order to protect the form and health of your longer-lived specimens. If you have very old trees that have seen better days, such as fruit trees or maples that have overly brittle branches or those that have accumulated lots of deadwood, they will never become attractive and should be removed without guilt.

4. **Deadheading and disfigurement:** Arborists continually struggle with those who insist on hacking back their fruitless mulberries and London plane trees each year to blunt, stubby branches. Not only is this unattractive, but is definitely unhealthy for the tree and generates more rank growth than normal. Some believe that deadheading was devised by unscrupulous tree trimmers who know that once the tree is cut back this way they will have an annual job of continuing the process indefinitely. When in doubt, remove deadheaded trees since they will never return to their original beauty.

The same applies to evergreens that have become misshapen by snow, overcrowding, or damage of any kind. Conifers, those evergreens with needled leaves, depend on their symmetry for beauty. Topping, removal of branches, or disease damage to portions of the tree can rarely be repaired, and rather than invest more time in such disfigurement, it's better to replace the tree with a new symmetrical healthy one.

Shrubs: The existing shrubs in your garden are the skeleton of the landscape. They are long-lived, sizable, and offer a variety of foliage, flowers, and colorful fruit. Older shrubs tend to exhibit certain problems related to their size and how well they have been cared for in the past. If oversized, they are usually sheared back to make

TREES AND SOIL PROBLEMS

Trees which originate in dry climates develop a means of reducing competition for what little soil moisture is available. These trees—including the black walnut, eucalyptus, and California pepper—exude certain oils from foliage and bark that are toxic to grasses and other small plants unfortunate enough to take up residence beneath the canopy. If one or more of these trees are present in your yard you may have already become discouraged with the poor performance of the small plants beneath or near them. Many people decide to create raised beds or to replace the surface soil to resolve the problem *temporarily*. But you may want to remove the trees altogether for a more permanent solution.

Oak trees and conifers can cause another type of problem. Their leaves are acidic, and when they fall and decompose beneath the canopy they make the soil more acidic. The ground under such trees can become so acidic that few plants will thrive except those that evolved to thrive on the forest floor. In addition, some species of oaks and conifers can have a dense layer of fine surface roots that make it very difficult to improve the soil. If these trees are growing in your yard you may be forced to make special provisions beneath them.

room for other plants or foot paths, or to clear adjacent patio space. This results in loss of their natural shape. Older shrubs tend to lose their lower branches, leaving the "legs" and the bare ground beneath exposed.

This is especially common among old junipers and other coniferous shrubs. It is tough, if not impossible, to remedy except by creatively pruning the plants into bonsai shapes. This can improve the appearance and allow light to penetrate through the branches so you can grow smaller plants to cover the ground below.

Shrubs repeatedly sheared over the years develop an outer shroud of green leaves while the inside of the plant is thick with dead twiggy growth. Big, overgrown broadleaf shrubs can look much better if carefully thinned from the inside out. This allows more light to enter the canopy, which stimulates a new flush of growth. It helps to water and fertilize shrubs after pruning to encourage new growth more quickly.

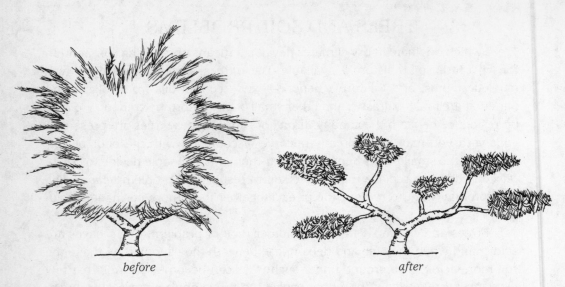

before   *after*

The best way to deal with old junipers or other shrubby needled evergreens that have lost their lower foliage is to creatively prune them in the bonsai style. This allows more light to reach the planting area beneath, where you can grow flowers in an area that had been too heavily shaded.

Shrubs with no potential may be removed entirely and replaced by more vigorous plants. The first year, you may want to fill in the gap with bushy annuals (described in chapter 3), but do consider a permanent replacement shrub better suited to the space.

Vines: Many vines such as honeysuckle and Carolina jessamine can mound up into nests of dead leaves and twigs. Only a fraction of this accumulation is actually supporting foliage since the nature of vines is to continually put out new runners on top of old. If the vine is thinned out and relieved of its dead twigs you will discover its original graceful growth habits instead of a dense bramble that has lost its architectural beauty.

You must be very careful going about this task since what may appear to be dead can support a flush of foliage at the tip. Therefore it's always better to work your way back from the far ends to the main trunk to avoid accidentally cutting the most prolific of the runners. Follow up your pruning with a good feeding and deep watering to encourage a flush of new growth.

Herbaceous Plants: "Herbaceous" is a general term used to describe all plants lacking woody parts. Herbaceous annuals and perennials should be seen as portable compared to permanent trees, shrubs, and vines that are too deeply rooted to transplant safely. This means that you do not have to work around annual or perennial bedding plants because they may be transplanted to other locations where they are more supportive of the new garden scheme.

These plants are the freebies of the shoestring makeover, and if they are perennials they may be divided into many extra plants in the process of transplanting. Identify and catalog how many of each plant you have at the start of the project and note what kind of exposure they have received in the past. Pot them up in order to get them out of the way while the renovation process is going on, then replant them where you wish. A budget gardener never buys a new plant when an older one can be coaxed into new vigorous life for free.

Lawns: When your kids are little the lawn is a place for them to play. Lawns also make our homes appear neat and tidy. But today, with water supplies growing more limited, concern over nitrate fertilizers increasing, and problems with clippings in the landfill becoming apparent, it's wise to reconsider your dedication to the traditional lawn. Chances are you may prefer a flower garden watered by a drip system or low-flow heads instead of a demanding lawn.

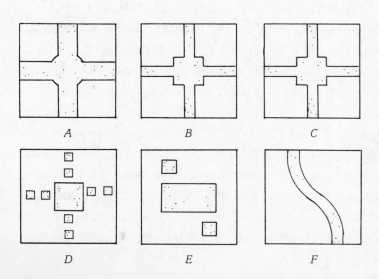

A *B* *C*

D *E* *F*

There are many ways to replace a tired front- or backyard lawn with a more creative layout using basic geometric patterns. These examples illustrate how paving, either poured-in-place or precast paving units, combined with flowers can transform a square patch of lawn into something special. Views A, B, and C are ideal for a bird bath or sundial at the center. View D utilizes precast concrete stepping-stones with a small slab at the center. Views E and F are ideal for slightly raised mounds to make the paving more natural.

Should you decide to keep your lawn, think about the amount of crabgrass or weeds that have taken up residence there. Are you ready to battle their invasions into the rest of the lawn or your flower beds? Look closely to see if the soil is overly compacted from kids, foot traffic, or vehicles, since this single problem is responsible for numerous turf grass ailments. Has there been so much buildup over the years that the level of the lawn has risen above the surface of the adjacent paving? This is very common in mild-climate St. Augustine grass lawns. Lawn restoration is difficult, but doable; see chapter 8 for details.

A Simple Test for Drainage: One of the most insidious problems in the garden is poor drainage. Muddy low spots are obvious, but subsoil drainage problems are the ones that come back to haunt you. Soil can be very deceiving because we see only the surface layer; deeper down, conditions may be exactly the opposite. It's not uncommon to find the soil surface dry and cracked while a foot down water is accumulating on top of very dense soil layers. This is very common in new subdivisions because the extensive grading required to cut and fill building pads may leave your house sitting on very dense subsoil that refuses to drain.

The problem you will experience with saturated soils is that water fills in all the little gaps between the soil particles, displacing for long periods of time the oxygen so vital to plant roots. Without oxygen the roots of most plants turn black, the outer skin peels off, leaving the entire system to rot away. Most people discover this problem only after they dig up the dead plants and find the roots smell like a cesspool.

Before you begin your makeover, it's wise to do a simple drainage test at one or more points around the yard. Get out the shovel and dig a hole that is at least two feet deep, but not necessarily very big around. In fact, a posthole digger is ideal for the task.

When you've finished digging, fill up the hole with water. If the water has drained away in an hour or two, you're in the clear. If it takes six to twelve hours, consider it slow draining. If there's still standing water after twenty-four hours, you've got a real problem that will impact trees and large shrubs with deep root systems. Under these conditions it's best to stick with shallow-rooted plants and water-adapted trees, because installation of underground drainage pipes is far too expensive a solution for budget gardeners.

PUTTING IT IN PERSPECTIVE

There are two reasons for such a detailed evaluation of all that exists around your home. The first is to get you thinking about each element, because when you take the tree or the fence or the flower bed out of the garden context and study it alone, you can be more objective about whether to improve, repair, or replace it.

The second reason is to help you see the spaces as a designer would, because design is a process, not a "thing." While you were cataloging everything, you became intimately aware of all sorts of little details. Perhaps you never noticed the ugly crawl space below the electric meter before, or that the lilac shrub has become mostly deadwood. Maybe you have always seen your trees collectively rather than the individual living things they actually are.

All this comes together later in chapter 5. There you'll actually measure and assemble what is to remain in order to draw a scaled base map of the raw, unimproved site. You will bring color, form, and character into this framework to ensure the shoestring makeover is intimately yours. But before you can begin designing your new garden, there is a lot of preparation you need to do—starting with getting organized.

CHAPTER 2

GETTING ORGANIZED

Get organized, develop a system, and stay consistent to the system.
Wisdom of the Budget Gardener

 The gardener's year is influenced by many things. The sun dictates the length of the day as seasons come and go. Weather patterns govern air and soil temperatures as well as rainfall. Farmers have long struggled to define and predict these variable conditions in order to coax larger harvests from their crops and orchards.

Gardeners also rely on all these elements, but it is usually frost that sets the greatest limitation to our own gardens. Whether it is the last cold snap of spring or the first frost in autumn, cold is the most important factor that slows and sometimes stops plant growth. Since the date of the last spring frost varies considerably between Minnesota and Florida, and can be very different from year to year, you'll have to guesstimate planting times.

Plants know their seasons far more intimately than we do. Their internal mechanisms are tuned to day length, soil temperature, and nighttime air temperatures. Plants sense subtle changes in light, soil, and cold long before they exhibit any external changes. Among the factors that will affect the growth of your plants and trees are:

Soil Temperature: Soil temperature is critical to seed germination. Summer annuals such as gourds, sunflowers, marigolds, and zinnias flat refuse to sprout when the soil is still very cool in spring despite warmer air conditions. In fact, sowing seed too early may cause them to rot in cold ground even if the last frost has passed. On the other hand, hardy cool-season plants such as sweet peas, bachelor's button, and some lettuces are reluctant to sprout in very warm soil. If they do manage to sprout, the heat causes the tender seedlings to wither promptly. For this reason, each annual plant described in the next chapter will be designated as either spring (cool soil) or summer (warm soil) to show you at a glance what soil temperatures are best for growing from seed.

It's often hard to know when the soil has heated up enough for summer sowing. To eliminate any doubt, purchase a soil thermometer from the nursery. It looks just like a meat thermometer with a rod you insert into the soil; the dial will tell you if it's warm enough to plant. It's worth the expense to buy a thermometer if you plan to do a lot of seed sowing for your summer garden.

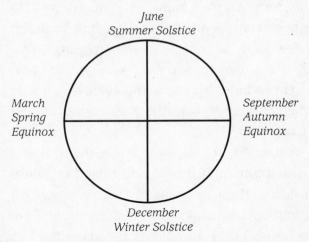

The gardener's year is broken down by four vital dates that relate to the position of the sun.

Day Length: Although our calendars designate the equinox as the "official" first day of spring, the actual date of spring's arrival as a season is really arbitrary. Spring is a period spanning several months during which the ravages of winter gradually abate and the first flushes of new growth appear. No matter where you live, the conditions of spring are highly variable. In some years those first signs come very late, and in other years they can come early to the very same location, extending the growing season well beyond normal. The big problem is that it's virtually impossible to predict such variations.

Summer also has a kickoff date, the solstice, which falls on June 21. This is the longest day and shortest night of the year, and begins a new annual solar cycle. From this point on, whether you realize it or not, nights begin to compose more and more of the 24-hour period. Plants of all kinds sense this point more than any other, and just a week or two after the solstice you may find the garden flowering and fruiting more profusely. That's because the plants have responded to those first shorter days by increasing attempts to reproduce.

Growing Season: Ancient farmers used preset dates for planting based on thousands of years of trial and error. This rigid approach is not always successful since nature is unpredictable, but it is the best we can do even today. With more accurate frost temperature data collected over the last century, the U.S. Department of Agriculture has put together some guidelines for the length of growing seasons to aid farmers. The growing season is the period of time between the average last frost of spring and first frost of fall and does not relate to soil temperature or day length.

To use the following Growing Season Table, choose the city closest to where you live. For that location you'll find the average length of the growing season. Consider that time as your window of opportunity for ideal gardening and entertaining. Do keep in mind that these frost dates are approximate and subject to some variation from year to year, and, just to be safe, allow a few days' leeway when making plans.

It's difficult to speak generally about such diverse climates, with growing seasons that range from just 150 days to year-round. Therefore, this book will divide the information into two categories—the short seasons of the North and the long seasons of the Deep South and Pacific Coast.

Short-season climates require fast-maturing gardens, and to suit them, many vegetable plant breeders have developed strains that flower and bear fruit more quickly to accommodate a short season. Often these annual varieties are described as "early maturing" because you can plant them late and harvest at the normal time. Another way to compensate for a limited season is to start plants ahead of time in a greenhouse, coldframe, or sunny window.

Short-season gardens also suffer the problem of repeated freeze and thaw as air temperatures gradually warm up. The ground freezes and expands, or "heaves," in the cold night air, then thaws out and contracts in the daytime. This soil movement is the primary cause of winter root damage, so protective mulches need to be applied not so much to keep out the cold as to minimize heaving. Cool-season gardeners must guard against the urge to plant on warm days during this freeze-and-thaw period, even if plants are frost hardy, because their roots can be damaged by heaving.

GROWING SEASON TABLE

City	Length of growing season (days)	Last spring frost	First fall frost
Albany, NY	169	Apr. 27	Oct. 13
Albuquerque, NM	196	Apr. 16	Oct. 29
Bismarck, ND	136	May 11	Sept. 24
Boston, MA	192	Apr. 16	Oct. 25
Burlington, VT	148	May 8	Oct. 3
Chattanooga, TN	229	Mar. 26	Nov. 10
Chicago, IL	192	Apr. 19	Oct. 28
Cincinnati, OH	203	Apr. 5	Oct. 25
Columbia, MO	198	Apr. 9	Oct. 24
Columbia, SC	252	Mar. 14	Nov. 21
Concord, NH	142	May 11	Sept. 30
Del Rio, TX	300	Feb. 12	Dec. 9
Denver, CO	165	May 7	Oct. 14
Des Moines, IA	182	Apr. 20	Oct. 19
Detroit, MI	181	Apr. 25	Oct. 23
Duluth, MN	125	May 22	Sept. 24
Eureka, CA	335	Jan. 24	Dec. 25
Evansville, IN	217	Apr. 2	Nov. 4
Fort Wayne, IN	179	Apr. 24	Oct. 20
Green Bay, WI	160	May 6	Oct. 13
Harrisburg, PA	201	Apr. 10	Oct. 28
Hartford, CT	180	Apr. 11	Oct. 28
Helena, MT	134	May 12	Sept. 23
Huron, SD	149	May 4	Sept. 30
Jackson, MS	248	Mar. 10	Nov. 13
Jacksonville, FL	313	Feb. 6	Dec. 16
Lander, WY	128	May 15	Sept. 20
Little Rock, AR	244	Mar. 16	Nov. 15
Louisville, KY	220	Apr. 1	Nov. 7
Macon, GA	252	Mar. 12	Nov. 19
Madison, WI	176	Apr. 26	Oct. 19
Marquette, MI	156	May 14	Oct. 17
Medford, OR	178	Apr. 25	Oct. 20
Midland, TX	217	Apr. 3	Nov. 6
Minneapolis, MN	166	Apr. 30	Oct. 13
Montgomery, AL	279	Feb. 27	Dec. 3
New Orleans, LA	302	Feb. 13	Dec. 12
Oklahoma City, OK	224	Mar. 28	Nov. 7
Omaha, NE	189	Apr. 14	Oct. 20
Parkersburg, WV	188	Apr. 16	Oct. 21
Phoenix, AZ	318	Jan. 27	Dec. 11

GROWING SEASON TABLE (*cont.*)

City	Length of growing season (days)	Last spring frost	First fall frost
Pocatello, ID	145	May 8	Sept. 30
Portland, ME	169	Apr. 29	Oct. 15
Portland, OR	279	Feb. 25	Dec. 1
Raleigh, NC	237	Mar. 24	Nov. 16
Rapid City, SD	150	May 7	Oct. 4
Reno, NV	141	May 14	Oct. 2
Richmond, VA	220	Apr. 2	Nov. 8
Sacramento, CA	321	Jan. 24	Dec. 11
St. Louis, MO	220	Apr. 2	Nov. 8
Salt Lake City, UT	203	Apr. 12	Nov. 1
Scranton, PA	173	Apr. 24	Oct. 14
Seattle, WA	281	Feb. 23	Dec. 1
Shreveport, LA	271	Mar. 1	Nov. 27
Spokane, WA	175	Apr. 20	Oct. 12
Toledo, OH	184	Apr. 24	Oct. 25
Trenton, NJ	211	Apr. 8	Nov. 5
Tucson, AZ	262	Mar. 6	Nov. 23
Washington, DC	201	Apr. 10	Oct. 19
Wichita, KS	210	Apr. 5	Nov. 1

Cities that are frost-free or experience only an occasional light frost: Los Angeles, CA; San Francisco, CA; San Diego, CA; Miami, FL.
Source: U.S. Department of Agriculture

Long-season gardens can be more difficult to define because the changes are not as noticeable. In fact, in areas like Miami or Los Angeles, flower gardens are possible all year around, with spring annuals planted in the fall to grow and bloom throughout the winter months. Where there is mild frost, hardy annuals are planted in late winter and bloom until the heat of summer slows them down (or until they're replaced by summer flowers).

Planning a makeover in long-season climates is fun because you can plant practically anything, but this makes choosing plants more complicated since there are so many choices. While short-season gardeners are stuck indoors during January and February, long-season gardeners are in the heat of spring planting. Here's how the two compare:

Long-Season Gardens
(more than 200+ days)

Short-Season Gardens
(fewer than 200 days)

September
   Plant spring seedlings outdoors.

September
Plant spring bulbs.

December
   Plant spring bulbs.

February
Sow spring annuals indoors.

February
   Sow spring annual seeds
      in garden soil.
   Sow summer annuals indoors.
   Plant summer bulbs.

April
Plant spring annual seedlings outdoors.
Plant summer bulbs.
Sow summer annuals indoors.

April
   Plant summer annual seedlings
      outdoors.
   Sow summer annual seeds
      outdoors.

June
Plant summer annual seedlings outdoors.
Sow summer annual seeds outdoors.

If your goal is to revamp your yard for a special occasion, take the time to study the table above. Should your home fall in an area with a growing season of less than about 200 days, then your choice of plants and the amount of time they will remain attractive and in bloom are limited. Under such constraints it is essential that you know the date of the event as early in the year as possible. If you have a flexible schedule, set the date at peak performance times. For the spring flower garden in cool climates, the later your date after the last frost the better. Similarly, the cool-climate summer garden is at its best around early August, just before plants begin going to seed.

Scheduling in long-season climates is not as critical. One difficult time is in the fall, when few plants are in bloom. The only other problem time is late spring, after your winter flowers have slowed down and the summer planting hasn't taken off yet.

Whether you are planning for an event in a short-season or long-season climate, the time needed for preparation and growing remains fundamentally the same. The key is to begin with your event date and then backtrack until you reach the earliest point you can work. Clearly this requires a well-prepared plan.

ORGANIZING YOUR PROJECT

List making is one of the most vital activities of any manager. Once an item or task is listed on paper, you need not remember it. The list does this for you. Lists can be reorganized all the time to keep them up-to-date as the project progresses. It's a good idea to buy yourself two notebooks: one that's the size of standard paper with a spiral binding, and the other small enough to keep in your back pocket. Use the little one to jot down notes when you're out in the garden, because by the time you get back indoors the idea may have vanished. Transfer information from the little notebook to the big one frequently.

TASK LIST OVERVIEW

The major tasks of a makeover are detailed in the following list, but they vary from yard to yard. The list will give you a sense of their proper order, to help you avoid the mistakes that are common to beginners. You'll have a much better idea of your actual tasks once you've prepared a more detailed plan, so refer back to this section when you're ready. In the meantime, the list provides you with a framework with which to view the project.

1. **Clean up, demolish, and remove.** Most yards look a lot worse than they really are due to long-term neglect. You may be pleasantly surprised at just how much improvement there is after you get rid of all the junk that's piled up out there. That means removing unwanted plants that are sick, damaged, or no longer beneficial to the landscape. Pull out weeds and any other unwanted plant material. Gather up all the litter, old woodpiles, broken toys, and paper. Sort through

TWO INDISPENSABLE SPECIAL TOOLS FOR EVERY GARDENER

The water wand is indispensable to any gardener because it allows you to surgically water tender young seedlings without damaging them. It's also a must if you have container gardens, particularly hanging pots and baskets that are watered overhead.

True budget gardeners should always be leery when it comes to buying specialized tools. But there are two that are indispensable for flower gardening and that you should budget into your project. First is the water wand. The water wand is sold under different brand names, but the products are all the same. This wand screws onto your garden hose and makes watering newly planted beds and containers much easier on both you and the plants. There are three parts to the wand: a fitting that screws onto the garden hose and includes a shutoff that allows you to turn off the water without going back to the faucet, which is vital for water-conscious gardening; a rigid aluminum rod that reaches into deep planters or above your head to hanging baskets; and, on the tip, a nozzle that diffuses the water pressure so it doesn't scour away the soil or push over little plants. Priced under $20, the wand is one of the most essential gardening tools you'll ever buy.

The other, although we usually do not like to use manufacturers' names in recommending products (since budget gardeners always shop around for the best generic prices), is the incomparable Miracle-Gro fertilizer system. Miracle-Gro is ideally suited to flower gardens because, as a water-soluble crystal, it is dissolved and applied in liquid form. But if you mix Miracle-Gro the old-fashioned way in a gallon jug or watering can, it can take all day to fertilize the garden. Since flowers need frequent light feedings, it's essential that you buy the Miracle-Gro proportioning gun, called "No Clog II." All you need to do is attach the gun filled with the dry crystals to the end of the garden hose, turn on the faucet, and water away. The gun automatically mixes the right amount of fertilizer into each gallon coming through it. Best of all, you can remove the gun's nozzle and screw your water wand onto the end for an extended reach! Sure, it costs a little more, but this is definitely an example of money well spent for a quality product.

all those useless building materials you've been saving for that "special project" and get rid of any that are unsalvageable. Chances are this stuff is so old and weather damaged you couldn't use it anyway.

Human nature is somewhat predictable, and we find that people notice what is out of order in a strange yard right away. But if you try to be equally as objective when viewing your own yard, it's likely you'll overlook quite a bit, since you've become so accustomed to seeing what's out there. It may be helpful to have a friend or relative over to point out what *they* find unattractive or what they see as junk.

Demolition is the teardown or tear out of dilapidated structures, fences, walls, and paving. Be careful how you do this because there are dozens of uses for scrap lumber and masonry, and if you're careless during teardown you may ruin their chances of being recycled. If you're removing a lot of shrubbery or trees, consider renting a chipper to grind up as much of the material as you can for mulch. Cut the larger pieces into firewood. All glass, paper, metals, and so on should be separated out and recycled. What's left can be hauled to the landfill.

You have three basic choices for transporting your unwanted backyard waste:

Cheapest: Put as much as you can in yard bags and hope the garbage truck takes it. Or haul the bags to the landfill in the trunk of your car.

Cheap: Dump everything into a rented trailer and haul it *en masse* yourself.

Expensive: Hire a hauling service to pick it up and dump at the landfill for you.

2. **Renovate and build.** All parts of the hardscape that remain need not be perfect. Before you decide to replace anything, remember, the theme of this book is to do it cheaply. Savvy budget interior decorators always recommend the "paint and paper" route for home improvement. In the landscape business, we use the "paint and plant" method. Repair what exists, apply a face-lift with paint and stain, attend to minor construction projects, and you can make a big difference. Just as you would paint before laying new carpet, so should you

make all your repairs, paint, stain, and build before you begin soil preparation or planting.

3. **Order plants.** Since every garden is different, you will have a personal schedule of what you need and when you need it. Chances are your local plant sellers won't have the exact plants you want, nor will they have sufficient quantities in stock. Therefore, the ordering process may occur over a long period of time during which you order, buy, and pick up your purchases only as they are needed. Do keep in mind that bedding plants that are fresh from the growers are always better than those that have been languishing in a retail store or in your own backyard for weeks on end waiting for you to get caught up.

4. **Gather the other stuff.** There are many other things you'll need for the makeover or party, ranging from red clay pots to fertilizer to loads of incidentals. Your plant list won't show these, so you need to develop a second list of nonplant items. If you are buying in quantity, don't forget to ask whether your supplier will extend you a quantity or bulk discount!

   This is the most difficult part to pull together since there is such a wide variety of materials options and design styles. To help you get all that you need, the following list includes many of the standard items that may be a part of your project.

Drip systems: Mainline, lateral line, emitters, filter, automatic timer.

Soil prep: Topsoil, compost, steer manure, limestone, fertilizer, peat moss.

Surface treatment: Weed barrier fabric, decorative ground bark, gravel mulch, wood chips.

Bed edging: wood, plastic, aluminum, brick.

Containers: pots, saucers, wire baskets, potting soil, sphagnum, hangers, pedestals.

Lighting: 12-volt outdoor lighting kit, strands of outdoor twinkle lights.

Optional tools: pointed shovel, flat shovel, leaf rake, bow iron rake, spading fork, hand trowel.

5. **Prepare and plant.** Depending on the scale and scope of your project, you may have more or less preparation to do before you plant. For example, anyone assembling moss baskets has much more to accomplish at the potting bench than in the garden. But thorough preparation of containers, soil, and irrigation ensure that you're rewarded with big, colorful, healthy plants that bloom and bloom and bloom.

     In the garden it is wise to do all your soil preparation at once, because this task is time consuming, requires special tools, and can be quite strenuous. It's also messy. If all the beds are ready at the same time, you can clean up, then ready all the seedlings, and go about the delicate art of planting them without interruption. The more quickly and smoothly your plants go into the ground, the sooner they will adjust and begin blooming. Try not to plant during heat waves or when dry winds are blowing, but when it's unavoidable, do so in the evening so the seedlings have all night to adjust.

6. **Feed and pick.** The two weeks after planting are the most critical as seedlings adjust to their new home. Spending a bit more time at this point means that the plants will be more healthy and durable later on. If you get a batch of plants that are poor growers through no fault of your own, go back to the seller and ask for replacements. Plant sellers strive to bring you only healthy, vigorous plants, and if their products fail to perform right away then chances are there was a problem with them before they left the nursery.

Thorough preparation is the key to success with any project, and it is particularly important in garden making because you are dealing with living plants that require special handling if they are to be successful in the long run. The program set forth in these pages is based on many years of experience encountering hundreds of mistakes by gardeners on all levels. One of the most common failings is the tendency to try and speed up the process by skipping what appear to be tedious, unimportant steps in planning. What some may fail to realize is that the steps are designed to make the gardener focus on certain details—the critical ones that, if neglected, will come back to haunt you later on.

CHAPTER 3

THE PLANT PALETTE

*Never plant just a pretty flower
when you can choose one
that's pretty and edible too.*
Wisdom of the Budget Gardener

 When you throw out all the lofty notions and rules of design, there remains only one clear goal of the process: to select the right plant for the right place. This means you must know the size, shape, growth habits, and solar exposure preference of a plant before placing it in your plan. Perhaps the greatest error you can make is to be swept off your feet by an emotional response to a plant based on flower shape, color, or fragrance. If you want a successful garden, these reactions must take a backseat to practical considerations that determine whether a plant will survive and perform in your garden.

If you were planning to paint a picture, you'd first choose a type of canvas, then the paint—acrylic, oils, or watercolor. Then you would assemble the colors that best represent the image you intended to reproduce. To an artist these materials and colors constitute the palette with which he or she will paint.

Garden makers do exactly the same thing when preparing to design a landscape. Their palette is a collection of plants that are suited to the project. Just as the artist doesn't use every single color at her disposal, you need not use every plant in your palette either. It simply provides you with a convenient collection of plants and flower colors to work with.

A plant palette can be broken down any way that suits you, but it is easier to organize it into basic categories that suit your goal: a fast makeover. The palette must consist of plants that mature and perform quickly—usually annual bedding flowers, biennials, fast perennials, annual vines, fast foliage plants, plus an assortment of bulbs. Every plant considered here will fall into one of these six categories, and the final palette will be organized this way at the end of the chapter.

It is important to use plants that you are familiar with, or those which grow well in your neighborhood climate. When in doubt, drive around to upscale hotels or shopping centers that are well landscaped and see what kind of seasonal plants their professional groundskeepers have used. Professionals tend to be very conservative about their plant choices because they cannot afford to risk a large-scale planting on unpredictable varieties.

In your travels, you may find a commercial landscape featuring a number of different petunia colors, and there are dozens grown today. When each of these colors were developed, they were given a name, yet few landscapers use them. Instead they tell growers what color flower they need—royal purple, for example—and they receive flats of purple petunias. You can use the same system for your own garden. It does help to understand how plants are named, though, if you find a variety you want to grow from seed yourself next year. That way you can scour catalogs for seed of the very same plant without guesswork.

Plant nomenclature can be confusing, so here's the long and short of it. Bedding plants have been bred to produce as many colors as possible from the same species of flower. When a new color is discovered, it is treated as a separate variety and given a specific name. Among sweet peas, for example, there are many shades of red, and each one is given a different variety name. "Pageantry" is deep burgundy, "Red Ensign" is scarlet, and "Superstar" is a deep pink. Commercial bedding plant growers usually stick with the most vigorous and reliable varieties of bedding plants for the immediate climate, which assures you the greatest chances of success. When you are lured in by oddball flowers based on luscious photos, you may not find them for sale at all, or, if you do, they may promptly prove why growers shy away from them.

The bedding plants profiled here are among those used most often by professional gardeners, but they are not the only ones at your disposal. We have ignored varietal names for the most part, since availability of local stock is the most crucial test. Some of the plants in our palette may have but one flower color, while others, like the pansy, offer almost every color in the rainbow. Watch for these rainbow plants if you're a beginner gardener; when you learn to grow one of them well, such as the petunia, you are assured an enormous color palette to work with.

ANNUAL BEDDING FLOWERS

These plants are the mainstay of the seasonal garden because they are naturally fast-growing, although sometimes short-lived. This is because an annual plant must sprout from seed, mature, and set new seed in a single season. A good number of the wildflower displays we see growing naturally in the countryside are annuals, which is why they have such a short period of color. Annual wildflowers must make seed for the second year's crop. Seed lying deep in the soil may germinate many years later if the soil is disturbed.

Long ago these wildflowers became domesticated and were specially bred to improve their flower size and coax new colors out of the gene pool. A wild woodland violet was bred to become a viola and pushed further by hybridizers to produce the big beautiful pansies so popular today. In addition, breeders have altered their size so that taller, rangy flowers are now accompanied by nearly identical dwarfed siblings and vice versa. All these improvements have turned a handful of staple bedding annuals into an enormous fast-and-cheap palette for makeovers.

The plants listed throughout this chapter are organized to provide you with the most essential facts about them and a short description of their use. Here are some details you'll need to understand before choosing among the listed plants:

Exposure: Most bedding plants need *some* sunshine, so even those indicated for shade may not perform well in deep, dark shade. If the plant is listed as "shade" or "part shade," it will take direct morning sun and filtered shade the rest of the day. "Part sun" flowers need lots of direct sun, but beware of unprotected exposure to hot afternoon sun and hot dry winds, because the long days of summer may force the plants to withstand these well into the evening hours. Flowers designated for "full sun" are heat lovers and may not perform at their peak unless given direct exposure all day long.

Flower color: Flowers that are just available in one color are indicated as such. Rainbow flowers are available in so many colors it's impossible to mention them all.

Since the list offers general information, be aware that, like the sweet pea example earlier, a flower designated as pink may have five different varieties of pink to choose from. Check availability before making your final choice.

Height: Flowers designated as "short" are well suited to planting as a floral carpet or in a border around other plants. They belong in the front portion of your planting to ensure they can be seen and are not blocked from view by taller plants. "Medium" flowers are often cutting varieties and the fillers of border plantings. They are big enough to make a bold planting statement but not so large that they take over. "Tall" refers to two types of plants. First are those that bloom in elegant spikes covered with many smaller flowers. These can be the most dramatic of all. If you pinch the tip off these spikes, or cut the flowers before they mature, the plant will respond by branching out. This lets you alter its shape somewhat if desired. Second are the big and bushy varieties that can attain the size of a mature shrub in just one season. These are useful for background, screening, and filling up empty space with just a few plants.

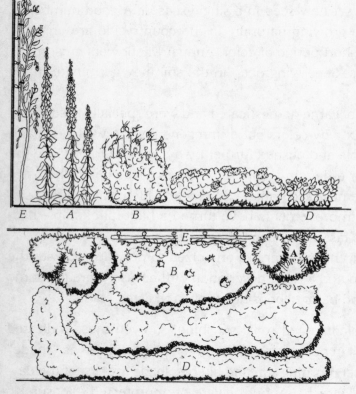

A. foxglove B. columbine C. impatiens D. wax begonia E. morning glory

Top view: *The heights shown for each plant in our palette help to determine where it should be placed relative to another. Each plant should be shorter than the one behind it so there is equal exposure to sunlight and the visual impact is of tiers of flowers.* Bottom view: *The same plants are arranged here to show how they are grouped into solid masses for brilliant color effects.*

Suitability: The way the flower is applied to or placed in the garden setting is important. This often is a function of its height and size, as described above. Some plants are particularly well adapted to containers, so look out for these designations if you're working with balconies, tiny spaces, or window boxes. Also watch for those identified as 2-for-1 flowers, which are both ornamental and edible flowers and are used more often today than ever before in *nouvelle cuisine* and as colorful garnishes.

Season: One distinction between flowers is their season of growth and bloom. Those designated "spring" will flower during the cooler days and take a light frost in stride. These will show a marked slowing in both vigor and bloom with onset of the hot season. The second group, designated "summer," are lovers of long days and heat, with their most vigorous growth phases occurring when soil and night air are sufficiently warm. These plants often prefer the dog days of summer to look their best, but die with the first cold snap of autumn. If you live in a subtropical climate with mild winters, some annual plants may become perennial, living for years without frost to kill them at the end of the first season.

Grow: This designation refers to the best way to start to grow the plant. Some plants, like sunflowers and gourds, sprout so readily from seed and grow so fast they can't be grown in containers. These are best sown directly into the ground where you want them permanently. Other plants are easy to grow from seed if isolated in their own containers, and most of these are available as nursery seedlings as well. And still more are finicky about their germination conditions and are best left to the professionals. These are often perennials sold like annuals and are best purchased from nursery-grown seedlings.

Diameter: Most of the plants will include a size designation indicating the diameter of that variety at maturity. This tells you how large an area is required to grow just one plant and how far apart to space the flowers in a planter. In general, the diameter is equal to the spacing of plants from center point to center point, not edge to edge. You must always lay out gardens according to mature size, not the size of the plant when you buy it at the nursery. Beware of stretching the space between plants too far since this may result in a skimpy garden.

The annual flowers listed below are the core of the seasonal garden. They bloom continuously if well cared for and can be encouraged to perform beyond their normal life span. Among these are many old favorites that have remained in growers' palettes since the nineteenth century because they are reliable and vigorous. There is quite a bit of variation among annuals, so be sure to note their differences.

Ageratum (*Ageratum houstonianum*)

Exposure: sun, part shade. *Flower color:* blue. *Height:* low. *Suitability:* edging, containers. *Season:* summer. *Grow:* from nursery-grown seedlings. *Diameter:* 8 inches.

This tiny annual is compact, will not sprawl, and bears blue flower heads shaped like broccoli. Controlled growth has made it an all-time favorite edging for walkways and around raised planters. Popular for container gardens because it will not overwhelm other small flowers, it is ideal for any garden where space is a concern. Its period of bloom is somewhat limited, however.

Bachelor's button (*Centaurea cyanus*)

Exposure: full sun. *Flower colors:* blue, red, pink, white. *Height:* medium cutting flower. *Suitability:* background, massing, individuals. *Season:* spring. *Grow:* from seed or nursery seedlings. *Diameter:* 14 inches.

A favorite old-fashioned, country-style cutting flower, the bachelor's button's muted colors and smallish flowers make it a great flower for late spring. Easy to sow right into soft garden soil, you can grow a big patch of them for pennies. If left to self-sow, it comes up again on its own the next season. The rangy growth habit of bachelor's button is not suited to small gardens or glitzy contemporary landscapes, but its charm, particularly for weddings, remains unmatched.

Begonia, wax or fibrous (*Begonia semperflorens*)

Exposure: shade, part shade. *Flower colors:* white, pink, red. *Height:* low. *Suitability:* edging, massing, containers. *Season:* spring/summer. *Grow:* from nursery seedlings or start your own plants from cuttings. *Diameter:* 8 inches.

There are hundreds of different begonias grown today, but these are the only ones considered bedding plants. Neat, compact growth habits make them ideal as edging or as a mass in the shade garden. There are three varieties: one with green leaves and white flowers, one with pink flowers, and the showiest of all with bronzed foliage and red flowers. Often all three are combined in extensive massed displays in public gardens. They will take a light frost and easily become perennial in mild climates. These begonias are fast and easy to root in moist sand. A larger, very popular variety, "Richmondensis," has magenta flowers atop glistening red foliage and is used frequently for the centerpiece of pots or hanging baskets, where it may live for many seasons if not exposed to frost.

Calendula, Pot marigold (*Calendula officinalis*)

Exposure: full sun. *Flower colors:* orange or yellow. *Height:* standard variety—medium; dwarf variety— low. *Suitability:* standards suited for backgrounds and cutting, dwarf plants for edging and massing. *Season:* spring and cool summers. *Grow:* from nursery seedlings. *Diameter:* standard 18 inches, dwarf 12 inches.

The absolutely easiest annual to grow, calendula is the marigold of winter and not related to the common marigold we see in summer. Calendula flower petals are edible and thus make a 2-for-1 plant, supplying blossoms not only for decoration but for garnish as well. It's a mainstay of winter gardens since it can withstand a considerable frost and still bloom when the days are short. Flowers are large, flat disks or daisies in yellow or orange. Dwarf plants are a reliable choice for massing, and taller standards should be staked since they tend to flop over in the rain.

California poppy (*Eschscholzia californica*)

Exposure: full sun. *Flower colors:* orange or yellow. *Height:* low. *Suitability:* massing and in areas where soil is poor or rocky but well drained. *Season:* spring. *Grow:* from fresh seed; sometimes available as nursery seedlings, but use care when transplanting as they do not like root disturbance. *Diameter:* 10 inches.

This eager little wildflower actually prefers poor soil as long as it is well drained. It makes an ideal treatment for hot dry embankments and rocky ground where traditional bedding plants fail. Rapid germination ensures a good crop of golden flowers in just a few months, so plant early. This poppy will sprout in cooler weather but dies back by early summer. Some new hybrids offer shades of red and pink but are not as vigorous.

Cineraria (*Senecio hybridus*)

Exposure: shade. *Flower colors:* white, pink, red, purple, blue. *Height:* low. *Suitability:* massing, container. *Season:* summer. *Grow:* from nursery seedlings. *Diameter:* 12 inches.

One of the few really bright flowers that will grow in the shade. Tidy, upright form and broad flower heads make them perfect for color masses where it is cool and moist. Plants die out quickly with onset of summer heat.

Columbine (*Aquilegia hybrida,* 'McKana Giants') (biennial)

Exposure: shade, morning sun. *Flower colors:* rainbow. *Height:* medium. *Suitability:* clusters. *Season:* spring/summer. *Grow:* from nursery seedlings. *Diameter:* 14 inches.

One of the most lacy and beloved plants native to North America, the McKana Giants strains are not only vigorous plants but bear very large multicolor flower clus-

ters. Foliage is remarkably similar to maidenhair fern but suffers mildew later in the season. Treated as an annual but technically a biennial, it dies out after the second or third year. Buy mature plants for assurance of a good showing the first year.

Cosmos (*Cosmos bipinnatus*)

Exposure: full sun. *Flower colors:* magenta, pink, white. *Height:* tall. *Suitability:* big, bushy plants large enough to become screening and hedge material. *Season:* summer. *Grow:* from seed or nursery-grown seedlings. *Diameter:* 24 to 30 inches.

Not for small spaces, cosmos is positively the biggest annual out there. A single plant, if well tended, can reach five feet in height and nearly as wide. Simple to grow from seed even by beginners, it simply loves hot, dry places if sufficiently watered. Sometimes cosmos plants become so large their own weight causes the stem to split apart. Avid growers provide elaborate staking systems to keep them intact as long as possible. This flower is a country-garden staple and a useful background for smaller, more fussy flowers.

Dahlia, bedding or border (*Dahlia coccinea*)

Exposure: part sun. *Flower colors:* rainbow. *Height:* low. *Suitability:* edging, massing, and containers. *Season:* summer. *Grow:* from nursery-grown seedlings. *Diameter:* 12 inches.

Do not confuse these little bedding dahlias with the huge perennials that grow from root tubers. Bedding dahlias exhibit all the color of their larger relatives but with a compact, yet upright growth habit. Flowers are stiff, vividly colored, and may cause more subtle flowers nearby to appear faded. It is best to combine these with potent blossoms such as pansies. Flowers turn to seed pods quickly unless you are diligent about keeping them nipped off. Plants do not grow well in very hot, dry conditions and prefer morning sun.

Iceland poppy (*Papaver nudicale*) (biennial)

Exposure: part shade, morning sun. *Flower colors:* red, salmon, orange, yellow, white. *Height:* medium. *Suitability:* massing and containers. *Season:* spring. *Grow:* from nursery-grown seedlings. *Diameter:* 8 inches.

Among the daintiest of flowers, these cups of crepe petals sit high atop thin, wiry stems. Technically biennials, they are treated as annual bedding plants that put on an incredible show for the early season. They will rapidly die out with the onset of summer heat and won't flower repeatedly like other plants, but when grown in dense masses, they are unbeatable. Iceland poppies are sensitive to root disturbance, so transplant carefully.

Impatiens (*Impatiens wallerana*)

Exposure: shade or morning sun. *Flower colors:* red, pink, white. *Height:* low. *Suitability:* massing, containers. *Season:* summer. *Grow:* from nursery-grown seedlings. *Diameter:* 12 inches.

Impatiens are queens of the shade garden and, though technically perennial in mild climates, they are treated like annuals everywhere else. Impatiens have become a popular filler among ferns and exotics due to their versatility and short, uniform growth habit. They also make ideal container color plants beneath patio awnings and shade arbors where few other bedding plants will bloom.

Larkspur, annual (*Delphinium colsolida*)

Exposure: full or part sun. *Flower colors:* mostly blue with less-common pink and white. *Height:* tall. *Suitability:* tall background and fillers. *Season:* spring. *Grow:* from seed or nursery-grown seedlings. *Diameter:* 12 to 14 inches.

Often confused with perennial delphinium, larkspur is strictly an annual plant which grows readily from seed. Its rangy character combines well with bachelor's button and columbine for a stunning late spring garden. Larkspur requires lots of space and may need staking later on, especially in partially shaded areas.

Lobelia (*Lobelia;* new species: *L. erinus*)

Exposure: sun, part shade. *Flower colors:* shades of blue from neon ultramarine to azure, with less-common rose and lavender. *Height:* low, cascading. *Suitability:* edging, containers. *Season:* summer. *Grow:* from nursery-grown seedlings. *Diameter:* 6 inches.

The undisputed favorite of the hanging basket crowd, this compact trailing plant literally can be covered with rich blue flowers that spill off pots like liquid amethyst. Simple to grow and nearly identical in habit to sweet alyssum, the two are often combined. When plants age and grow leggy, shear them back gently with scissors to encourage a new crop of luxurious flowers. Lobelia will bloom continuously even through the longest growing seasons, and if it threatens to die back, give it a good haircut, then water and fertilize heavily for a new flush of growth.

Marigold, African (*Tagetes erecta*)

Exposure: full sun. *Flower colors:* yellow, orange. *Height:* standards tall, dwarf medium. *Suitability:* massing, cutting, containers. *Season:* summer. *Grow:* from seed or nursery-grown seedlings. *Diameter:* standard 18 inches, Solar Series 14 inches.

Do not confuse this plant with the pot marigold native to Europe. This flower is native to Latin America and was brought back to the Old World, where its current form was developed in gardens of Northern Africa, hence the name. The taller variety has pompon-shaped dense blossoms the size of a baseball, and has long been banished to the cutting garden because the flowers are so top-heavy the plants frequently split apart or flop into the mud when wet. Recently the "Solar Series"—new, short varieties of African marigolds—have become widely available, with the same big flowers on stubby plants that let them back into the main garden as excellent candidates for masses and edging.

Marigold, French (*Tagetes patula*)

Exposure: full sun. *Flower colors*: yellow, orange, red/bronze. *Height:* low. *Suitability:* massing, edging, containers. *Season:* summer. *Grow:* from seed or nursery-grown seedlings. *Diameter:* 10 inches.

Probably the most widely recognized and versatile flower in today's garden, these marigolds were brought from the New World to France, where they were crossed over and over again to yield a variety of flower colors and shapes from little pompons the size of a golf ball to single daisies in red and orange. Their small stature makes marigolds a must for summertime pots and window boxes as well as massed plantings. They adapt to almost every need, are naturally heat resistant, and bloom vigorously even during the late summer when other flowers are withering.

Marigold, pot. *See* Calendula.

Pansy (*Viola wittrockiana*)

Exposure: sun, part shade. *Flower colors:* rainbow. *Height:* low. *Suitability:* massing, edging, and containers. *Season:* spring/summer. *Grow:* from nursery-grown seedlings. *Diameter:* 8 inches.

In mild climates pansies will grow and bloom throughout the winter and are replaced by more heat-tolerant bedding plants in time for summer. But pansies are a summertime love of cooler-season gardeners because they can be adapted to almost every condition in the garden. Few other flowers can rival the incredible array of color in pansies; from pure white to black, magenta to gold, they are all beautiful and make some of the finest container flowers. These giant flowers are so close to the ground they are often spattered with mud and cannot hold their faces up under the weight of water from sprinklers. They are popular for pots and hanging baskets where they are protected, and are better appreciated up close.

Periwinkle (*Catharanthus rosea*)

Exposure: sun, part shade. *Flower colors:* white, pink, red. *Height:* low. *Suitability:* massing, edging, and containers. *Season:* summer. *Grow:* from nursery-grown seedlings. *Diameter:* 6 inches.

The dark green foliage of periwinkle and its carefree nature make it a favorite with beginners. The plants themselves are not fancy, but neat uniform growth like that of dwarf marigolds makes them one of the best fillers for formal and semiformal gardens. The plants are not particular about soil and will tolerate considerable shade. Their reliability has made them popular in commercial building courtyards and entries.

Petunia (*Petunia hybrida*)

Exposure: sun. *Flower colors*: rainbow. *Height:* low. *Suitability:* massing and containers. *Season:* summer. *Grow:* from nursery-grown seedlings. *Diameter:* 14 inches.

The petunia rivals the pansy as America's favorite bedding flower, but the petunia is much more heat tolerant. The trumpet-shaped blossoms are vivid in every color of the rainbow. Hybrid flowers that range from a plain single trumpet to those packed with petals with ruffled edges offer more than just rainbow colors. Their casual growth habit allows petunias to spill off containers or over walls, and they will ramble as they age to cover quite a bit of ground. They are susceptible, however, to a variety of caterpillars.

Primrose (*Primula polyantha*)

Exposure: shade. *Flower colors:* rainbow. *Height:* low. *Suitability:* edging, massing, containers. *Season:* spring. *Grow:* from nursery-grown seedlings. *Diameter:* 8 to 10 inches.

Frequently called English primroses to distinguish them from the dozens of other members of the primrose family, these are the most boldly colored of all primroses, with clear hues that are uncommon in woodland shade gardens. Primroses bloom once in early spring and therefore may not be the wisest choice if you're looking for a long bloom period. Technically perennial, in most climates they are treated as annual bedding plants. They are best used as edging, in containers, or anywhere they won't get lost amidst larger plants.

Scarlet sage (*Salvia splendens*)

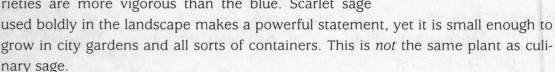

Exposure: sun. *Flower colors:* red or blue. *Height:* medium. *Suitability:* massing, edging, containers. *Season:* summer. *Grow:* from nursery-grown seedlings. *Diameter:* 12 inches.

This versatile spiked annual bears bright red-orange flowers that will bloom off and on all season. The red varieties are more vigorous than the blue. Scarlet sage used boldly in the landscape makes a powerful statement, yet it is small enough to grow in city gardens and all sorts of containers. This is *not* the same plant as culinary sage.

Snapdragon (*Antirrhinum majus*)

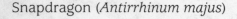

Exposure: part sun. *Flower colors:* rainbow. *Height:* standards tall, dwarf low. *Suitability:* background, cutting. *Season:* spring. *Grow:* from seed or nursery-grown seedlings. *Diameter:* standard 14 inches, dwarf 12 inches.

Snapdragons offer very large, showy flowers during the spring when temperatures are still cool. They are one of the simplest tall flowers to grow and come in

many different potently colored strains, though most are in the pastel range. Do not place vivid flowers like scarlet sage beside snapdragons as they may overwhelm these more subtle colors. Stock (described below) and bachelor's button are far more complementary. The standards may require staking since flowers tend to be top-heavy. Dwarf snapdragons, with their compact growth habit, offer the same flowers in a more manageable plant ideal for pots, hanging baskets, and those little pockets of earth in city gardens.

Stock (*Mattiola incana*)

Exposure: full sun. *Flower colors:* white/cream, pink, purple, blue, red. *Height:* tall. *Suitability:* background or massing. *Season:* spring. *Grow:* from nursery-grown seedlings. *Diameter:* 14 inches.

Stock is an old-fashioned flower that is making a comeback due to its sweet fragrance, a rarity in annual flowers. It grows initially into a single spike, but once this is cut it will branch out like a candelabra and bloom again with smaller flowers. It's a natural for spring gatherings and weddings because of its soft pastel-colored flowers. It tends to slow down with the onset of summer heat, however.

Sunflower (*Helianthus annus*)

Exposure: full sun. *Flower colors:* yellow, red, white. *Height*: tall. *Suitability:* background fillers. *Season:* summer. *Grow:* from seed. *Diameter:* 36 inches.

Everybody thinks the mammoth sunflower is the only strain of this beautiful summer plant, but there are many smaller-flowered varieties that are fast growing and delightfully countrified. The red and multicolored varieties have daisylike blossoms about the size of your hand that make fine cutting flowers. The more these are pinched back the more numerous but smaller the blooms. Since they literally spring up from seed in warm ground and mature in such a short time, use them to mask ugly spots or neglected corners, and be sure to save the seed for planting an even bigger patch next year. You can expect the standard mammoth sunflower to grow to well over ten feet tall and bear a single flower up to two feet in diameter. These are all heavy feeders, and if watered and fertilized well, they will outperform everything in your garden. Another 2-for-1 plant, the sunflower is not only ornamental but the seeds are edible, making a fine wild-bird food.

Sweet alyssum (*Lobularia maritima*)

Exposure: full sun. *Flower colors:* white, purple, pink. *Height:* low. *Suitability:* edging, masses, containers. *Season:* summer. *Grow:* from seed or nursery-grown seedlings. *Diameter:* 12 inches.

Alyssum is so eager to grow that it is essential to the container gardener's plant palette. Low growing with a trailing growth habit, it is perfect for edgings. Available only in white or purple, use sweet alyssum to fill in spaces between larger plants in a new landscape, and, if conditions are right, they will self-sow for years to come. Since alyssum seems to prefer sandy, very fast-draining soil, hanging baskets give it the perfect opportunity to perform. Alyssum is enhanced when combined with the blue lobelia which shares a nearly identical habit.

Viola (*Viola cornuta*)

Exposure: part sun. *Flower colors:* purple, white, yellow. *Height:* low. *Suitability:* edging, massing, containers. *Season:* spring. *Grow:* from nursery-grown seedlings. *Diameter:* 8 inches.

These modest predecessors of the modern pansy are smaller flowered but more versatile since their blossoms don't flop over when they get wet. Although there are many strains of viola, the clear-colored flowers are the most charming and vigorous. A popular variety called Johnny-jump-up is used in early spring baskets because of its cascading habit, similar to that of the summer flowers lobelia and sweet alyssum. This is another 2-for-1 plant because the flowers are a very popular garnish among connoisseurs of *nouvelle cuisine* and were salad favorites during medieval times.

Zinnia (*Zinnia elegans*)

Exposure: full sun. *Flower colors:* rainbow. *Height:* tall. *Suitability:* cutting, massing, background, containers. *Season:* summer. *Grow:* from seed or nursery cuttings. *Diameter:* standard 18 inches, dwarf 12 inches.

The zinnia has no competition when it comes to pure potency of color; it is so bright that some seem as though they should glow in the dark. Here is a big bushy annual that rivals the finicky perennial dahlia for flower size and is capable of withstanding the intense heat of desert gardens. Perfect for cutting, it will bloom repeatedly until frost and is most welcome during late summer when little else is in bloom. Bold enough for mass backgrounds, zinnias are a staple wherever summers are long, hot, and dry.

PERENNIAL BEDDING FLOWERS

Perennials are favorite flowers of the experienced gardener, who knows that their long life span and increasing size make them a good investment in the long run. Unlike annuals, which explode with growth and bloom profusely over a long period, perennials are slower to get started and bloom for a limited period of time. The consolation is that perennials, unlike annuals, need not be replanted from scratch each year.

Some perennials are exceptions to this slow-to-start rule, however, particularly in mild climates, where they are everblooming until frost. As a result, it can be difficult to classify some perennials, particularly those native to tropical climates. But a few are perfect for garden makeovers because they grow fast and bloom profusely in a single growing season.

Because we are focusing on short-term garden makeovers, the plant profiles that follow will be only those which promise high performance the first season. Many of them are grown and sold in six-packs like annuals, but you may find the very same plant in a larger container with a hefty price tag. Knowing that these are frequently grown in six-packs ensures that you can obtain the greatest number of long-lasting plants for the lowest price. Note also that perennials that remain in the ground through the winter require special protection in cold climates. Winter protection is basically the insulation of the underground root system against the repeated freeze-thaw of soil, which causes lasting damage.

Aubretia (*Aubretia deltoidea*)

Exposure: full sun. *Flower colors:* purple, red. *Height:* low, cascading. *Suitability:* rock gardens, containers, flower beds. *Season:* spring. *Grow:* from nursery stock. *Diameter:* 12 inches.

Aubretia is a favorite in Britain, where it adapts to crevices in old stone walls in which there is little soil to trap moisture. This condition points to aubretia's preference for very fast-draining soils. It behaves like a perennial alyssum and will bloom repeatedly during the growing season if cut back frequently with scissors to discourage seed production. Aubretia hasn't caught on here in the States yet, but is perfect for areas such as the Pacific Northwest, which has frequent summer rain.

Black-eyed Susan (*Rudbeckia hirta*)

Exposure: full sun. *Flower colors:* yellow, orange, brown. *Height:* tall. *Suitability:* background, filler. *Season:* summer. *Grow:* from nursery-grown seedlings. *Diameter:* 20 inches.

Black-eyed Susans are big, vigorous, reliable, and make a fine cottage garden plant. Fully perennial, they will grow each spring on the same roots, but eventually may be divided into many new plants. Often sold as an annual flower because it is quick to mature and bloom the first year, the plant, in fact, does much better the second season. Plants can exceed four feet in height and become bushy enough to serve as fillers along with cosmos, annual larkspur, and zinnias. A dwarf variety is available, so check the labeling of nursery seedlings carefully.

Daisy, Euryops (*Euryops pectinatus*)

Exposure: full sun. *Flower color:* yellow. *Height:* tall, bushy. *Suitability:* background, filler, hedge, container. *Season:* summer. *Grow:* from nursery stock in cold climates, seedlings in frost-free zones. *Diameter:* 36 inches.

Similar in size and character to the marguerite, this plant is also a shrublike perennial that grows large in a single season, particularly if planted from two- or five-gallon container stock. In warmer areas it is long-lived enough to last a few years if gently pruned to encourage new growth and prolific flowering. Beginners make the mistake of planting too many of these, which results in a yellow monochromatic garden.

Delphinium (*Delphinium elatum*)

Exposure: part sun. *Flower color:* blue. *Height:* tall spike. *Suitability:* high-impact bedding areas. *Season:* spring. *Grow:* from nursery-grown seedlings. *Diameter:* 14 inches.

No other flowers are as majestic when in bloom as delphiniums, but these are demanding perennials that don't look their best until the second season. For a fast garden effect, buy them as two-year-olds in one-gallon containers, and be sure to stake bloom stalks for support. Mulch, water, and feed them after they bloom in spring to ensure a second showing in early fall. Delphiniums are not recommended for beginners.

Dusty miller (*Senecio cineraria*)

Exposure: full sun. *Foliage color:* silver. *Flower color:* yellow. *Height:* medium. *Suitability:* background, accent, containers. *Season:* spring/summer. *Grow:* from nursery-grown seedlings. *Diameter:* 18 inches.

Dusty miller is grown chiefly for its beautiful silver-gray foliage that provides a beautiful contrast to a background of deep green. This gray foliage literally glows under a full moon and has become popular for planting with the contrasting sand-dollar-shaped, lime-green leaves of nasturtiums. Its flowers are very small yellow daisies. It is often used as a filler for container gardens because of its natural vigor and the startling way it adds dynamics to color pots. Keep in mind, however, that this is an accent plant: a little is good, a lot is disastrous!

Foxglove (*Digitalis purpureus*)

Exposure: part shade, morning sun. *Flower colors:* pink, purple, cream. *Height:* tall spike. *Suitability:* background, bedding areas, clusters. *Season:* spring. *Grow:* from nursery- grown seedlings. *Diameter:* 14 inches.

   This is actually a biennial plant that blooms best in its second season. Foxglove is often treated as an annual because it will put forth a modest flower spike the first year. One of the most beautiful flowers for the shade garden, foxglove may need staking. It should be planted in dense clusters for best results. **Note: All parts of this plant are poisonous: keep away from children, pets, and livestock.**

Fuchsia (*Fuchsia hybrida*)

Exposure: shade. *Flower colors:* pink, red, white, lavender, coral. *Height:* low, cascading. *Suitability:* containers. *Season:* summer. *Grow:* from nursery stock. *Diameter:* varies.

   Few plants have as many hybrid varieties and such beautiful flowers as the fuchsia. It is primarily a hanging-basket or container plant because the flowers are pendulous like earrings and must hang freely to look their best. Therefore, fuchsia baskets are usually hung so that the flowers are at about eye level. Fuchsias are not commonly mixed with other plants because they can grow so big. Growers have come up with an exceptional flower-bed fuchsia variety called "Gartenmeister Bonstedt," which is very upright in growth and bears lovely bronze foliage and lipstick-red tubular flowers that are a favorite of hummingbirds. Fuchsias are not frost hardy, so in cooler climates gardeners store their fuchsias while dormant for the winter in a dark place protected from cold. Come spring they are brought out again to be fed and watered back to life.

Geranium, zonal (*Pelargonium hotorum*)

Exposure: full sun, part shade. *Flower colors:* many shades of pink, red, white. *Height:* medium. *Suitability:* containers, bedding. *Season:* summer. *Grow:* from cuttings or nursery-grown seedlings. *Diameter:* 16 inches.

To avoid confusion, you need to know there are two main types of bedding geraniums. Zonal geraniums are the upright growers with round fuzzy leaves, while the second type, ivy geraniums, grow in a trailing habit. Everyone's grandmother loved zonal geraniums, which were often grown in a sunny window or on the porch because they aren't frost hardy. Zonals are fast-growing and equally fast to root from cuttings. Thirty years ago they were favorite trading materials among garden club members so that all shared the latest in these neon flowers. There are no better plants than geraniums for pots because they grow so quickly and you need not combine them with other plants for a good show. A row of red clay flower pots overflowing with an assortment of geranium flowers is one of the most charming and cheap accents you can create. Plus, at the end of the season, you can bring them indoors to bloom in a sunny window throughout the winter.

Hollyhock (*Alcea rosea*)

Exposure: full sun. *Flower colors:* rainbow. *Height:* tall spike. *Suitability:* background, bedding areas, clusters. *Season:* summer. *Grow:* from seed or nursery-grown seedlings. *Diameter:* 14 inches.

This flower is the favorite of country gardeners due to its ability to grow from seed even in hot, dry places. Big and brilliant, hollyhock bloom stalks can grow to be over eight feet tall, and so they are quite visible as background flowers. In some settings the hollyhock becomes so top-heavy it falls over, which is why you see them often growing against fences, building walls, and porch railings where they can be tied up securely. Foliage at the base of each stalk is not attractive, so be sure to plant some smaller flowers around the bottom as camouflage. Hollyhocks show best their second season and self-sow prolifically if allowed to go to seed.

Marguerite (*Chrysanthemum frutescens*)

Exposure: full sun. *Flower colors:* white, pink, yellow. *Height:* tall, bushy. *Diameter:* background, filler, hedge, container. *Season:* summer. *Grow:* from nursery stock in cold climates, seedlings in frost-free zones. *Diameter:* 36 inches.

In the mild southern states or California, the perennial marguerite is so large it is treated as a shrub. These plants are prolific, but in frost-free zones their life span is limited to about three to four years. Where winters are colder, the marguerite can be planted as a seasonal annual from larger sizes of nursery-grown stock, such as two- or five-gallon containers, for instant flowering shrubs. For a backyard wedding, a healthy supply of marguerites can become the framework of the garden, set off by surrounding multicolored annuals.

FAST VINES

Vines are the great cover-ups of the garden. They cover ugly fences, barren walls, sheds, and anything else they can climb upon. Annual vines can grow a startling amount in just a few months. The gourd, a relative of squash, is a rampant climber and has the ability to shroud an entire fence line in foliage or cover a shade arbor. In frost-free or mild climates annual vines such as the morning glory can take on massive proportions.

Each vine has its own means of climbing. Some, such as the gourd, have specialized tendrils that wrap around anything they can reach. With others, the main stem twines itself around the trellis. Many simply bear a trailing growth habit that cascades off walls, or that may be draped over a fence or used as a cover-up, but which have no way to adhere on their own. Remember that a vine with nothing to climb on becomes a groundcover capable of covering large embankments or open spaces in a flash.

This group of plants may prove to be the most useful for those trying to meet a deadline. Since many of those listed grow very well from seed, they are also an inexpensive way to cover, screen, shade, and cloak virtually anything. When grown in baskets, some make very attractive hanging plants beneath patio covers or tree canopies, with long tresses of foliage able to reach the ground in just a few weeks' time.

Gourd (*Langenaria siceraria*)

Exposure: full sun. *Flower color:* white. *Size:* big, very large leaves. *Suitability:* shading foliage, self-clinging with tendrils. *Season:* summer. *Grow:* from seed.

If you can grow winter squash, you're guaranteed success with gourds. There are many types, from those little warty ones you find in the supermarket to huge African kettle gourds. Among these is the group known as langenaria, which designates the larger bottle gourds most often called "birdhouse" or "dipper." The seed for birdhouse and dipper are most widely available, grow attractive vines with big leaves, and produce useful fruit and white flowers. A single main runner can stretch thirty feet or more along a fence line or across a roof, and blooms with white flowers that open at dusk. These runners produce a few female flowers and lots of male flowers on each plant; if you are growing for the fruit, pinch back the main runner to encourage more female flowers to sprout on the lateral runners that result. If you want fewer gourds and more vegetative growth, leave the end tip intact. Be sure the soil is very warm before planting gourd seeds as this is critical to both germination and early growth rate.

Ivy geranium (*Pelargonium peltatum*)

Exposure: full sun, part shade. *Flower colors:* white, pink, red. *Size:* small/medium. *Suitability:* embankments, bedding plants, hanging baskets, containers. *Season:* summer. *Grow:* from cuttings or nursery-grown seedlings.

Ivy geranium is a bright green trailing plant with flowers similar to those of its sister, the zonal geranium. It is best planted in raised planters or hanging baskets where its long limbs may trail gracefully and bloom over the entire length. In frost-free climates, this plant is clearly perennial and grows to gigantic proportions. But where there is frost, ivy geraniums are treated as annuals. At the end of the season, pot them up and bring them indoors for the winter, then propagate more plants from cuttings in time for next year's planting. Ivy geraniums are also used as a groundcover and on slopes in warm climates, where they will live for many years. Like most vines, ivy geraniums should be fed and watered heavily for ideal performance.

Morning glory (*Ipomoea tricolor*)

Exposure: full sun, part shade. *Flower colors:* blue, purple. *Size:* medium. *Suitability:* cover-up, groundcover, twining, hanging baskets, climbs by twining stems. *Season:* summer. *Grow:* from seed (soak for 2 days first).

Morning glory is a favorite old-fashioned vine that grows rampantly from seed, engulfing entire houses and cloaking big trees in southern California and Florida. It bears attractive medium green leaves in profusion that are later studded with vivid violet-blue trumpet flowers. Your plants may or may not produce flowers the first season. Morning glory can be invasive, as is its wild relative, called bindweed, because it can strangle other plants by curling itself around them. Few plants, however, can rival the beauty of the electric-blue blossoms, but if you grow morning glory from seed, be sure to read the instructions on the packet; the seeds require some scarification and soaking before you plant them in the ground.

Nasturtium (*Tropaeolum majus*)

Exposure: full sun, part shade. *Flower colors:* yellow, red, orange—all on same plant. *Size:* small. *Suitability:* groundcover, containers, trailing plant. *Season:* summer. *Grow:* from seed or nursery-grown seedlings.

Nasturtium bears some of the most beautiful leaves in the plant kingdom, and even if it never bloomed, the plant would still remain popular for its lovely rounded foliage. Nasturtium is a 2-for-1 plant because the petals are a spicy and colorful addition to salads or as a garnish. It prefers the cool season or coastal conditions and makes a fine, fast-growing groundcover in just one season.

Scarlet runner bean (*Vigna caracalla*)

Exposure: full sun. *Flower colors:* purple/red. *Size:* small. *Suitability:* wall or fence cover-ups, hanging baskets, climbs by twining stems. *Season:* summer. *Grow:* from seed.

This is a showy member of the common bean clan and is grown as an ornamental even though the beans are edible. Just as with all pole-type beans, it must have something to climb on and is as easy to flower as any edible bean variety. Nineteenth-century gardeners favored it as a quick source of color, and after gradually falling out of favor it is now making a comeback. Scarlet runner bean is a summer plant, quick to germinate in warm soil. Although it is growing popular for *nouvelle cuisine,* the seed companies still list it as an ornamental.

Sweet pea (*Lathyrus odoratus*)

Exposure: full sun. *Flower colors:* rainbow: *Size:* small. *Suitability:* cutting flowers; cover-up for the faces of walls, fences, screens; climbs by tendrils. *Season:* spring. *Grow:* from seed (presoak in warm water).

Sweet-pea flowers emit a charming fragrance, but these colorful vines are not very large and suffer with the onset of summer heat. They are ideal for cool-season gardens and will bloom repeatedly over many weeks if well cared for. Tendrils require very small mesh trellises similar to the plastic netting for covering fruit trees. This netting is cheap to buy in large quantities; just cut it to a suitable size, staple it onto a wood fence, or hang it between two poles, where it becomes practically invisible. **Note: All parts of this plant, flower, seed, and greens, are poisonous.**

Verbena (*Verbena peruviana*)

Exposure: full sun. *Flower colors:* purple, pink, magenta-red. *Size:* medium/large. *Suitability:* very flat ground-cover. *Season:* spring/summer. *Grow:* from nursery- grown seedlings or flats.

When landscapers want a new job to look good immediately, they plant verbena to fill in the spaces between young shrubs and perennials. Very heat- and drought-tolerant, verbena is a reliable cover-up for abandoned play areas and vacant vegetable plots. This potent flowering species remains just a few inches tall but each plant grows to nearly three feet in diameter or more. One flat of plants can fill in a huge area with color if planted at spacings of about two feet, and it will cost you only pennies. While sensitive to heavy frost, verbena is low-growing enough to be mowed for a neater appearance after early summer flowers fade. Water and feed well for a second flush of growth and more flowers.

INSTANT PLANTS FROM ROOTS AND BULBS

When you think of bulbs, consider each one as a tiny package that contains one full-grown plant. Quality bulbs, not those puny cheap ones you can buy for pennies, are some of the very best sources of fast color since they are already two or three years old. Bulbs are also highly versatile because they can be forced to grow and bloom out of season. The downside of using bulbs is that they bloom just once a season, and for a limited period of time. No amount of coaxing will force a tulip to bloom again in the same season, while a marigold may be encouraged to bloom repeatedly for months on end.

Bulbs, like annuals, are divided into two groups: the frost-hardy spring bloomers, and the tender bulbs that flower in summer. Most summer-flowering bulbs cannot survive the winter in cold or frozen ground and thus should be treated like seasonal annual plants. Most bulbs are dug up at the end of their season, divided and stored to ensure big vigorous flowers the following year.

Spring bulbs which resist the cold are the early season lifesavers; little crocus will pop up out of the snow and narcissus can begin flowering in January if it is mild. All bulbs are well adapted to container gardening and are versatile, because you can put them on hold in the refrigerator until the designated time for a special party or date.

Not all plants we loosely call bulbs are true bulbs. An onion is a true bulb, with its many layers or "scales." Daffodils and most of the spring bulb clan are true bulbs. Others are technically corms, such as gladiolus and anemone, but these are planted no differently than true bulbs, with the rooting end facing downward. Corms are much harder to the touch than true bulbs, and benefit from a few hours' soaking in warm water before they go into the ground.

Forcing bulbs is a popular technique which exposes spring bulbs to artificial spring conditions to make them grow and bloom out of season. This is a trick used by swanky nurseries to tempt their more affluent customers into paying many times the cost of a bare, fully dormant bulb. This same trick is at our disposal and offers everything from front porch color to spring garden party centerpieces for a tiny fraction of what the fancy retailers charge. Step-by-step instructions for forcing bulbs are detailed in chapter 7.

Bulbs are best bought from catalogs during the dormant season and are easily shipped through the mail. You'll be able to choose from an incredible array of varieties and colors which far exceeds that of any garden center. Buying bulbs in bulk directly from growers or distributors guarantees the lowest price possible.

Anemone

Exposure: full sun. *Flower colors:* rainbow. *Height:* 12 inches. *Suitability:* containers, massing. *Season:* summer bulb. *Grow:* from corms.

The best way to use anemones is to plant them in drifts of mixed colors. Each corm should be four to six inches from the next to ensure even color without unsightly gaps. It helps to soak the dry corms in warm water for an hour or so before planting. Anemones are sometimes mixed with ranunculus for variety since they are similar in size and coloring.

Daffodil, Jonquil, Narcissus

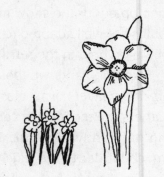

Exposure: full sun. *Flower colors:* yellow, white. *Height:* to 18 inches. *Suitability:* massing, containers, cutting. *Season:* spring bulbs. *Grow:* from bulbs.

Most people can't tell a jonquil from a narcissus, but suffice it to say they both bear flowers similar to the common daffodil's but in different sizes and colors. These bulbs are the absolute simplest way to inject masses of color and fragrance into the awakening garden. In mild climates these plants can bloom as early as January. Where it is much colder they will survive year after year in garden soil. Daffodils that have developed colonies act more like wildflowers and are considered "naturalized." This is partly because they are among the few bulbs not gobbled up by gophers, and may naturalize into colonies living for nearly a century. Flower size varies considerably among the dozens of varieties, with the big golden yellow King Alfred daffodil the showiest of all.

Gladiolus

Exposure: full sun. *Flower colors:* rainbow. *Height:* to over 36 inches. *Suitability:* background, cutting. *Season:* summer bulb. *Grow:* from corms.

The gladiolus is one of the most unappreciated plants, probably because it is so cooperative the garden world takes it for granted. The colors offered by a multitude of hybrids guarantee the impatient gardener a treasure trove of cutting flowers and tall background perennials at bargain basement prices. These plants tend to be top-heavy, so be sure to insert stakes deep into the soil at the bottom of the planting hole as bulbs are planted to ensure they are stable enough to hold these beautiful flowers. Keep in mind that gladiolus spires may be cut before blossoms open, then placed in water where they will gradually open over many days. If bulbs aren't lifted and separated at the end of the season, gladiolus may not bloom well or true to color the following season.

Ranunculus

Exposure: full sun. *Flower colors:* rainbow. *Height:* 12 to 15 inches. *Suitability:* containers, massing, cutting flowers. *Season:* summer bulb. *Grow:* from dry root clusters.

These fully double flowers of poppy-thin petals are almost neon in hue and, when grown in large masses, they are quite striking. Each bulb produces one, perhaps two, flowers at the most, so spacing between plants should be about six inches for a bold, continuous effect. Ranunculus are often combined with anemone and make fine cut flowers, so be sure to grow a few extras.

Tulip

Exposure: full sun. *Flower colors:* rainbow. *Size:* varies widely, showiest varieties reach 30 inches tall. *Suitability:* all-purpose—containers, cutting, massing, accent. *Season:* spring bulb. *Grow:* from bulbs planted in fall or very early spring.

Tulips seem too easy to grow considering the delicacy and potent coloring of these flowers. But grow they do, in dozens of different types ranging from just ten inches tall to the giant Darwin tulips. Tulips are always most dramatic when you grow lots of them, and it's a common mistake of beginners to just set out a few bulbs and then regret not being more generous. Gophers just love tulips, so beware if they are a problem in your yard. Tulips can be disappointing the second year if they were not lifted out of your garden and given proper care before replanting the following autumn. Mild climates lack enough winter cold to force dormancy, so tulips are unlikely to grow or bloom the second year.

PATIO TREES

In recent years growers have developed new container stock known as "patio trees." These aren't really trees but shrubs that have been trained to a single trunk with a nice round foliage head. Patio trees are designed specifically for container culture and are absolutely charming in small-space gardens. A matched pair can flank gateways or stand at the corners of a swimming pool. When added to steps or just about any other semiformal application they are always dramatic, and you can plant the soil around the base of the little trunks with flowering annuals for even more color.

Flowering patio trees offered by a major California wholesaler, Monrovia Nursery, include an assortment of azaleas, camellias, gardenias, hibiscus, crape myrtle, and raphiolepis. They also produce some fruit trees in this form that are both ornamental and productive, including a wide variety of citrus. Other more hardy patio trees produce colorful berries, such as the hollies, cotoneaster, and pyracantha. And of course there are privets for topiary and more exotic junipers for Asian themes.

Growing a tree in a pot is no more difficult than growing any other plant in a container except that it may eventually outgrow the space allotted for the root zone. Should you choose to grow trees in pots, be sure to stick with species that are small in stature, such as Japanese maples, crape myrtle, dogwood, and laurel. These will attain a size no larger than their roots can support, and all take to creative pruning to keep their forms looking good on a small scale.

Citrus patio tree
in five-gallon container.

Camellia patio tree
in five-gallon container.

PRETTY FOOD

We tend to separate our food plants from garden flowers, yet both complement one another in the ornamental landscape. Today's creative gardeners plant edible greens and vegetables in the same way we use bedding flowers. In these versatile gardens you're likely to find red peppers among the zinnias and chives nestled in alyssum. Among these plants are other decorative strains such as burgundy red-leaf lettuce and the gourmet favorite, radicchio.

People are growing their own food plants because our menus emphasize unusual salad greens, fresh herbs, and vegetables. If you've priced those lovely baby-lettuce salad mixes at five to ten dollars a pound you know the problem. For what you spend for one bag of delicate greens you can buy a six-pack of gourmet lettuce seedlings or a few packets of seed that will feed you throughout the entire growing season.

City gardeners have always grown a few edible plants in their ornamental landscapes simply because there isn't space for a separate kitchen plot. To supply the needs of these urban customers, growers have developed miniature versions of much larger plants, such as patio tomatoes, bush beans, miniature "Bambini" eggplant, and dwarf cucumbers. Today the demand has shifted to plants that are naturally sized for small flower beds or window boxes.

City gardeners will find some winning combinations of dwarf vegetable plants in chapter 4, on container gardening. But for those just starting out, the vast assortment of greens and gourmet edibles in catalogs can be overwhelming. To simplify matters, the following list comprises plants that are fast-growing, small in stature, and big in flavor. They are separated into three main categories: herbs, salad greens, and colorful edible flowers (see Nasturtium, Scarlet Runner Bean, and preceding section, Pretty Food).

HERBS

There's always a lot of confusion over exactly what constitutes an herb. Technically, the term herb is short for herbaceous, which means the plant lacks wood and is made up of soft green stems and leaves. But we know bay leaves are grouped with herbs, yet these are borne on a full-sized tree. Thus, the term herb applies to more than just soft green plants.

The herbs we use today in the kitchen are a combination of annuals and perennials, with a few exceptions that are biennial, such as parsley, which die out in the second or third year. The most commonly grown annuals, such as basil or cilantro, grow easily from seed. Perennial herbs like rosemary and sage live for many years. Some perennials may be grown from seed, but germination can be so slow it may be worthwhile to buy them as nursery-grown seedlings.

The best culinary herbs for instant gardens or container gardens adapt to a wide variety of dishes while offering attractive foliage and flowers. Those listed here may be available in an assortment of varieties that bear variegated foliage or other qualities that make them more suited for the ornamental planter.

Basil (*Ocimum basilicum*) (annual)

Exposure: full sun. *Height:* 30 inches. *Landscape value:* lime-green or bronze. *Flowers:* pale flower spikes. *Grow:* from seed or nursery seedlings.

Standard basil varieties grow tall by the end of the season. Nip off the tips to discourage flowering and force a more compact habit.

Chamomile (*Anthemis nobilis*) (perennial)

Exposure: full sun, part shade. *Height:* 14 inches. *Landscape value:* spreading carpet. *Flowers:* pretty white daisies in profusion. *Grow:* from seed or nursery seedlings.

Once you have chamomile in the garden, you need never replant it again. Lovely cascading plants covered with white and yellow flowers spill over container edges. Shape occasionally with scissors to remove spent flowers and encourage a new flush of growth.

Chives (*Allium schoeonoprasum*) (perennial)

Exposure: full sun, part shade. *Height:* 14 inches. *Landscape value:* singles or edging, and unusual leaf shape. *Flowers:* lavender pompons on stiff stems, edible. *Grow:* from seed, bulbs, or nursery seedlings.

Chives grow from little onionlike bulbs into tufts of long, narrow leaves, and when the flower stems bloom they are very attractive plants. Small size makes them perfect for containers and they look cute when grown in a row around the edges of a pot.

Coriander, Cilantro (*Coriander sativum*) (annual)

Exposure: full sun. *Height:* to 30 inches. *Landscape value:* background. *Flowers:* small, white. *Grow:* from seed or nursery seedlings.

Coriander is a foliage plant treated much like basil. Its leaves are bright green, and later, when plants bolt and bloom, they are topped with delicate umbels of white or pale pink flowers.

Mints (*Menta spp.*) (perennials)

Exposure: part shade. *Height:* to 24 inches. *Landscape value:* groundcover. *Flowers:* each type slightly different; flowers borne on spikes are lavender, pale blue, white. *Grow:* transplanted cuttings from existing stands, or start with nursery seedlings.

Mints are lovers of cool, moist conditions and there they grow vigorously. Foliage is a lovely deep green, and plants are eager to spread out like a groundcover.

Oregano (*Origanum heracleoticum*) (perennial)

Exposure: full sun. *Height:* about 12 inches. *Landscape value:* single or groundcover. *Flowers:* white and insignificant. *Grow:* from nursery seedlings.

Oregano is a low-growing plant that roots like a groundcover as it spreads. Produces a lovely carpet of foliage that will spill off container edges and fill up a pot in no time.

Parsley (*Petroselinum crispum*) (biennial)

Exposure: full sun, part shade. *Height:* 16 inches. *Landscape value:* edging. *Flowers:* insignificant. *Grow:* difficult to germinate seed, grow from nursery seedlings.

As a biennial, your parsley will flower and die at the end of its one- or two-season life span. Once it bolts to flower, plants are no longer attractive and should be replaced.

Rosemary (*Rosmarinus officinalis*) (perennial)

Exposure: full sun. *Height:* standard to 30 inches, dwarf to 14 inches. *Landscape value:* single or groundcover. *Flowers:* blue, purple. *Grow:* from nursery seedlings.

Rosemary is a very long-lived plant and is a vital part of the dry gardens of the West. The standard variety can grow quite large, so for container gardens request the dwarf variety, 'Prostratus.' Dwarf rosemary is a groundcover that grows well in a pot if planted around the edge, so that it can spill downward.

Sage, garden (*Salvia officinalis*) (perennial)

Exposure: full sun. *Height:* to 20 inches. *Landscape value:* singles. *Flowers:* purple spikes. *Grow:* from nursery seedlings.

Garden sage is the most widely grown culinary *Salvia*. Its soft-textured, gray-green or variegated foliage provides the opportunity to contrast with deeper greens. Tends to cascade somewhat if planted on walls or in pots.

Thyme (*Thymus vulgaris*) (perennial)

Exposure: full sun, part shade. *Height:* 15 inches. *Landscape value:* edging, groundcover. *Flowers:* small and insignificant. *Grow:* from nursery seedlings.

Common thyme is a cascading plant that looks its best only when it's hanging off the edge of a pot or wall. It is easy to grow, and you can renew aging plants by cutting them back and following up with plenty of water and fertilizer for luxurious, dark-green growth.

GREENS OR LEAF VEGETABLES

Most quality salad greens that are attractive in gardens are annuals and perennials. Lettuce, the largest group, is an annual, so you may grow it among your spring and summer garden flowers. The best lettuce varieties for ornamental gardens are those classified as "leaf" or "loose leaf" forms, which are large tufts of upright-growing leaves rather than dense round heads. Many leaf lettuces have bronze-colored leaves, such as 'Fire Mountain,' described as a deep burgundy, with leaves deeply lobed like those of an oak tree. These less common lettuces, with their lovely foliage and unique leaf shapes, offer you a versatile alternative to strictly ornamental foliage plants.

A trough packed with gourmet leaf vegetables, or, better yet, a patch of them in the flower garden, provides lovely foliage and organically grown, freshly cut greens at your fingertips. Leaves of seedlings and mature greens can be harvested with scissors so plants live longer. Since these plants provide great foliage for backgrounds or borders, those with bronze coloring such as radicchio, red cabbage, and red leaf lettuce add even more spice to the planting scheme. The popular ornamental kale sold as a bedding plant is edible, as is its highly ornamental relative escarole, with its frilly, variegated leaves.

There is but one thing you must know to successfully grow greens. A typical leaf lettuce plant grows into layers of succulent large leaves, but when the temperatures warm, the plant senses the time to flower and set seed. To do so, the lettuce bolts, which means that the central stem of the plant elongates into a flower stalk, much the same way a foxglove does. Once the lettuce has bolted, it isn't particularly beautiful and the quality of the greens declines quickly. Damp, cool coastal environments are ideal for greens to grow large and luxurious before they bolt. If you live in a hot climate, premature bolting can be such a problem that some greens are simply out of the question.

There are many attractive salad greens that aren't lettuce but that grow in a similar way. Some are eaten fresh while others are cooked, and all grow far better in cooler climates. These plants aren't always available at local nurseries, though, so you'll probably have to start them from seed. Following are four ornamental greens in categories that encompass numerous varieties to choose from:

Endive (*Chichorium endive*) (annual)

Height: short.

The chief characteristic of endive is the frilly leaf edges that make the heads so beautiful you'll hate to cut them for salads.

Kale (*Brassica spp.*) (annual)

Height: tall.

Plants are covered in blue-green leaves and are closely related to broccoli. They're tolerant of heat and will live through mild winters, providing year-round edible background foliage.

Radicchio (*Chichorium iutybus*) (annual)

Height: short.

The lovely heads are wrapped in cabbagelike leaves that are pure white and veined in bright red.

Swiss chard (*Beta vulgaris cicla*) (annual)

Height: tall.

Upright plants, lovely foliage color, and a very long life span make this green a desirable part of every garden. Plant singly or as background.

The plants presented above include annuals, perennials, vines, bulbs, herbs, and leafy greens for your flower beds. Do not feel you should know them all, because it is a rather large list. A good way to narrow down the options is to read through the plant information on the list and use a red pencil or highlighter to mark those you recognize and would like to grow. This will help you start your working plant palette with core materials you are familiar with.

To take the process a step further, explore some new plants, but just one or two at a time. Go to the library and look them up in a plant dictionary that has color photos; then look for them at a nursery. Don't be afraid to experiment with new plants, because the facts provided about them here are enough to ensure your success. Remember, you learn much more about plants by what you do wrong than by what you do right, so do not be afraid to make a mistake. No matter how much gardening experience you have, there is always something new to learn.

CHAPTER 4

CONTAINER GARDENING

Reliable meat-and-potato flowers always outperform unproven gourmet varieties.
Wisdom of the Budget Gardener

 Creating gardens in containers brings flowers where there is no earth and foliage where there is no place for trees and shrubs. It is the salvation of the city gardener who is limited to a single window, a balcony, or a tiny courtyard.

About thirty years ago, a revolution in techniques moved gardening beyond the basic one-plant-in-a-pot concept. While the art world was tuning in to psychedelic color schemes, California nurseries were applying this rich palette to container gardens. Bowls, traditional flower pots, troughs, and hanging moss baskets were stuffed with a riot of annual flowers that transformed a patio from mundane to exciting in minutes.

Pots filled with blooming color are the most versatile elements for instant makeovers. Containers eliminate the hard work of soil preparation. They are also much easier to maintain in the long run because you need not struggle with weeds or litter, and plants are right at your fingertips when you need to nip off spent flowers.

Even though container gardening is easy and convenient, it can be very expensive. Just take a look at the prices on Italian terra-cotta pots at many nurseries to see just how pricy it can become. Where you need only buy plants and a bag of compost to plant directly in the ground, container gardening requires many purchases, which can add up to quite a sum. New gardeners may be forced to buy many items just to get started, including the container itself, pedestals, drip pans, potting soil, and plants. If you are using a do-it-yourself drip irrigation system, there is even more to buy. To keep your container garden makeover within a reasonable budget, you must be a smart planner and savvy shopper. Planning ahead and knowing exactly what you need is the best way to ensure low-budget success.

CONTAINERS

There are many ways to use containers when creating gardens, and virtually all will fall into one of the categories that follow. The key to success is in choosing the right container style to match the size and character of your space. Then the plants should be carefully considered in order to ensure they grow in your local climate and are well suited to the exposure the container will receive. We look at plant containers in three different ways: their size, the material they are made of, and their value in terms of planting and design.

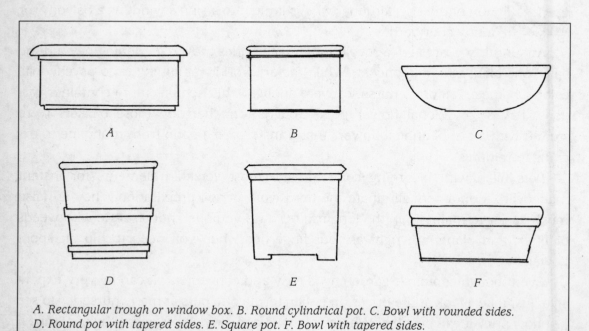

A. Rectangular trough or window box. B. Round cylindrical pot. C. Bowl with rounded sides. D. Round pot with tapered sides. E. Square pot. F. Bowl with tapered sides.

Window boxes and troughs: A window box is attached to the building just below a windowsill. Most window boxes are composed of an outer shell that is visually attractive and permanently attached to the wall with brackets. They are made of steel, wood, ceramic, or cast stone, and designed so that the drainage doesn't shed back toward the wall where it can cause staining.

The actual planting is done in a second plastic box of similar size that sits hidden inside the decorative outer shell. This lets you plant the window box elsewhere, then carry the finished product to the window and set it inside the shell. The two-box system is also helpful during winter, when the entire inner shell can be removed and stored until it's time to replant in spring.

Troughs are nearly identical to window boxes but sit directly on the ground. They were originally made of stone or clay, and became popular for growing culinary herbs on the tiny balconies of nineteenth-century Parisian apartments. Troughs remain ideal for balcony gardens and fire escapes because they use space most efficiently. Long and narrow, they can be pushed up against the base of a railing or wall. Round pots may hold just as many plants, but the circular shape requires nearly twice the patio or balcony space.

Sometimes troughs are set upon ornamental bases or blocks for improved drainage or for better visibility. Raised troughs look beautiful when planted with cascading flowers. In England, troughs carved from a single block of stone were used for laundering and animal feeding hundreds of years ago, and are so durable they have survived the ravages of time and are now coveted by gardeners. More sophisticated designs of cast stone or terra-cotta clay exhibit attractive outer textures to mimic wicker basket or classical Greco-Roman designs. Troughs range from 18 to 40 inches long or more, depending on the manufacturer, and can weigh up to 200 pounds if cast in clay or stone. Plastic troughs are now widely available and weigh substantially less.

Bowls: These shallow but wide containers are specifically designed for seasonal color because there is insufficient rooting depth for longer-lasting plants. Bowls are typically used in spacious areas where other containers are too small to exhibit a sizable mass of color. Big bowls are difficult to handle once planted due to the weight of soil and moisture, not to mention their unwieldy shape. They also require more frequent watering since the shallow soil heats up and dries out quickly with so much surface area. Bowls need to be flooded daily to give enough moisture for rapidly blooming plants, and are best irrigated by hand or with a circular drip ring rather than individual drip system emitters.

Round pots or vases: This is the largest of all the container groups because it includes the standard flower pot, the monster containers used in corporate office buildings, and everything in between. Quality varies considerably as does the ornamentation around the outside. In the old Italian villas, it was common to plant citrus trees in giant terra-cotta pots that were moved indoors to glassed *orangeries* during the cold winter months. This ability to plant small trees in large containers has kept the big pots in style among urban gardeners because they provide the opportunity to grow trees for fruit, shade, screening, and accent even where there is no soil. Ideal for balconies, terraces, and overly hot decks or patios, these pots can exceed three feet deep and over 40 inches in diameter. Beware of their weight, because when planted they can be quite heavy.

Square pots: Even though they can be expensive, the exotic oriental character of square pots is readily apparent, and those designed with little feet are even more elegant. Deep enough for very large plants, these pots are perfect when pushed into corners and planted with small trees or large tropical plants. Square pots combined with rectangular troughs provide the greatest amount of planting area without sacrificing precious people space.

Urns: These were all the rage in the classical gardens of the Roman Empire and remained in use until Victorian times. Urns are shaped somewhat like a wineglass, consisting of a pedestal topped by an open bowl of varying depth. These containers tend to appear out of place in most modern gardens because they project such a formal, if not gothic, character. Beware of these unless you are planning a toga party or creating a specific effect, as they are expensive and can look tacky when out of place.

Decorative cachepots: When houseplants are used by interior decorators, they typically leave the plant in its nursery pot and slide it into a more attractive glazed ceramic or porcelain cachepot. This is not just a decorative choice; the cachepot has a solid bottom which acts like a drip pan to collect moisture that would otherwise stain the tabletop. Just as the window box is placed inside an ornamental shell, you can use all sorts of ornamental containers as outer sleeves or cachepots to disguise functional pots.

For example, you'd never plant directly into a colorful olive oil tin because it would quickly rust and lose its beauty. But you can place a nursery pot *inside* a tin and achieve the very same effect. This also applies to containers made of galvanized metals, copper, silver, pewter, and brass that would rust or corrode if filled with potting soil and water, which work perfectly when used as a sleeve.

Wire moss baskets: These are perhaps the most popular container for growing hanging plants. They consist of a wire mesh basket with grids about two inches in size. The baskets come in a wide variety of sizes including "half baskets" that are shaped so they can be flush mounted directly onto a fence or wall. The basket is lined with moss, and into this nest the potting soil is placed. Sphagnum moss is highly absorbent and provides a layer of moist insulation around the root zone, which ensures it will always be well drained. Perhaps the best quality of these moss baskets is that you can not only plant into the open top, but also through the sides, so that the entire basket is covered in flowering plants.

Material Characteristics

Until recently containers were almost always made of red terra-cotta clay, but clay has some drawbacks that should be considered before you invest in it. While it is a porous material which absorbs water and allows a healthy exchange of air through the pot walls, this characteristic also causes moisture loss, which is not good for gardeners who have a severely limited water supply. In addition, when the moisture moves through the walls of a clay pot it can leave an ugly staining or white mineral buildup on the outside, marring its beauty. Unless you use special acids to clean these pots they will discolor, particularly if your water supply contains high levels of salts. To reduce this evaporative potential and ensure that all the moisture given to the plant remains where it can be readily used by the root system, use more dense stoneware pots or those with outer glazing that blocks the transfer altogether.

Despite all the drawbacks, many gardeners still cling to red clay because it is so beautiful, yet professional plant growers now strictly use plastic pots. In fact, there is no problem with using plastic, and it may make plants grow better as long as they aren't overwatered and are planted to ensure adequate drainage. To satisfy the demand for red clay while offering the low cost and water retention of plastic, you'll find plastic pots that appear identical to terra-cotta in most of the styles detailed earlier. And plastic is lightweight and does not discolor on the outside.

The downside is that some plastics weaken under long-term exposure to sunlight and extremes of temperature. While smaller pots hold up better than large ones over the long run, the plastic may become exceptionally brittle. Although there is no visible sign of change, just try to move one of these containers after it's been sitting a year or two and you may find the whole thing breaks apart as soon as it is lifted. The better-quality and more expensive pots have special inhibitors in the plastic to make them stronger. Cheap pots may last one or two years at most if kept outside year-round, which may not be a problem if you're planning a preparty face-lift on a strict budget.

Redwood once was used widely to make pots because it is resistant to decay, but over time even the best of these will disintegrate. Today, fuchsias and other hanging pots are frequently sold in wood containers because they keep the soil inside well aerated. These are attractive enough to stand on their own, although you can paint or stain them as you wish. One of the best deals around are the oak half-casks used by the liquor industry, which are large enough to hold a small tree, and the outer slatted surface and metal bands need no additional finishing. Eventually these too will rot out.

Wood is the ideal material with which to make the outer shell of window boxes or sleeves for nursery plant containers since these can be made to size with only a few special tools. Homemade redwood containers, however, are no longer a do-it-yourself project because the price of lumber has skyrocketed. Pine and fir are more cost-efficient materials, and the outside surfaces of containers made out of these two woods can be painted to match a house or stained to bring out the natural-wood grain. If you are artistic, virtually anything from hearts to ivy garlands can be painted on wood shells without the need for special primers.

CAVEATS

Whenever you place a pot flat onto paving, the drainage hole on the bottom may not function properly. If it is blocked off, the pot won't drain adequately and the soil will sour, turn black, and smell bad. These conditions will drown and rot the roots of any plant. This is often the case with very large, heavy pots, particularly those made of plastic, because there is no moisture loss through the pot walls. We don't move these pots around very often, so signs of poor drainage remain undetected until it's too late.

For this reason you'll want to put a spacer under the pot to lift it up slightly; this will allow the drain hole to work more effectively. You can try little squares of ¼-inch or ⅜-inch plywood at three or more points around the hole, but these will rot away after a while. The best and cheapest solution is to obtain free samples of ceramic tile at a local showroom, preferably those that would be thrown out anyway. Square two-inch tiles are ideal for smaller pots; use larger sizes for big pots. If you can't get little tiles, break up larger ones. A single Saltillo terra-cotta tile can be broken into enough shards to serve a few pots. To gain more space under the pot you can stack up the tiles to the desired height.

Improper drainage can also be a problem when using cachepots. The functional container inside will drain into the cachepot, and if it's not emptied, water can collect at the bottom. You can reduce the chances of this happening by placing a layer of gravel or shards in the bottom of the cachepot so that the inner pot is raised up to allow the extra water to evaporate.

Containers of any type that will sit on a patio or deck will stain the surfaces beneath them. On a concrete patio, accumulated moisture can provide an environment for algae to grow and extend into the porous paving. These green or black stains are very difficult, if not impossible, to remove. Wood decks are particularly susceptible to rotting from moisture concentrated in the wood beneath the pot or drip pan. No matter where you place your containers, it is essential you include drip pans on your shopping list, then move them around from time to time to release the moisture trapped beneath.

The large ceramic saucers that go with terra-cotta pots can be very pricy, but hold up indefinitely unless they are dropped or a pot is dropped on the saucer. Some poor-quality red-clay products can stain concrete paving simply due to prolonged contact and moisture. These can be replaced with the clear plastic pans that are nearly invisible and do the job well, but unfortunately, these pans can become overly brittle after a while and fall apart.

Keep in mind that container gardens are portable, just like art or indoor accent furniture, so you can rearrange them to your heart's content until the look is just right. Take full advantage of this flexibility because it is out of the question with permanent garden plantings. You will find more information on plants for containers in chapter 3, and how to design them into your plan in chapter 5. Detailed planning is essential to the success of any container gardening project, and if you follow the suggestions throughout this book from plant selection to planting and aftercare, you are guaranteed a lush, blooming garden in the most unlikely places.

MAKING PLANS

Design the corners and the rest takes care of itself.
Wisdom of the Budget Gardener

Remember the old saying: "If you clean in the corners the rest takes care of itself"? This is particularly appropriate for gardening since it illustrates how important the details are to the overall visual quality of any space, indoors or out. Even though budget gardeners are not architects, you can still give your yard the same level of detailed attention that you would an indoor room. Look into that corner by the back fence and the narrow sideyard along the garage wall. All you need to do is to open your eyes and stop long enough to notice the little things. In fact, this is an ideal excuse for spending a lot of time out in the yard sipping coffee or a cocktail, because the mind functions much more creatively when we are at rest.

DESIGN

Landscape design is a process, but since our goal is short-term, low-cost, and high-impact change, we can bend the rules considerably. This is particularly true when dressing up a yard for a special event since the time frame is so limited. The process is a bit more involved for a garden makeover since you may be planning long-term improvements while immediately implementing the single-season concepts. Nonetheless, look at a garden face-lift in the same manner you would when redecorating a room. First consider the spaces, then note the permanent elements that exist there, and finally—the best part of all—create and install your new look.

It is next to impossible to create any kind of garden without a plan. Plans give us a better understanding of color distribution and spatial relationships, and help us visualize the final product. But most of all, they are important estimating tools without which you have no way to tally the number of new plants and materials you will need. Since we're working within a budget and time frame, it's important to draw the house and the planting areas correctly. The house and boundary lines of your lot are the most permanent part of the homesite, and they will ultimately dictate where and how planting areas are arranged on your plan.

STEP 1—HOUSE AND LOT FIELD SKETCH

To begin, you'll need a measuring tape, a blank piece of paper, a pencil with an eraser, and perhaps a helper too (measuring goes a lot more smoothly if there's someone else to hold the end of the tape where it's supposed to be while you record the data). Consider taking some snapshots of the yard before you begin. Shooting many different angles helps you remember all the nooks and crannies of a site when it comes time to design. If you aren't visual, the photography is doubly important.

The goal at this point is to gather information in the form of measured dimensions. To begin, first sketch out the house at the center of your piece of paper. The sketch does not have to be to scale, but each wall should be shown clearly enough to produce a drawing that actually resembles the shape or "footprint" of the house. Since windows and doorways are the links between indoors and out, show these on the sketch as well, but again, they do not have to be exact. You will be applying a dimension to each of these openings, so be sure they are clearly marked. A simple way to do this is to draw each segment of wall in a much heavier line than that for windows and doors.

The most important part of the line you draw is the point where it starts and where it stops. This applies particularly to the point where walls intersect doors and windows. Once you have drawn all walls, windows, and doors on the footprint, each segment may be measured. Write down the measurement beside each segment, expressed in feet and inches (for example, 5′ 6″).

Your house exists inside the boundaries or property lines of your lot. With the house sketched on your sheet of paper, you may tie down its position on the lot. In most cases, though, there will be a fence, sidewalk, or alley to mark the edge.

With the lot lines sketched around your house, take at least one, preferably two, measurements from wall to property line on every side. For example, lightly draw a line on your paper extending from the north wall of the house to the north property line. Now measure from the house to the property boundary in roughly the same place. Write the resulting dimension beside the sketched line. Repeat the same process on all sides of the house to tie down each boundary accurately.

Between the house and property line there are other things which should be a part of the plan. Among these are fences and gates, paving, walls, ponds or pools, arbors, gazebos, and other outbuildings. Be sure you locate and measure outdoor electrical plugs, air conditioning condensers, faucets and sprinkler valves, coal chute, and any overhead utility lines. These may or may not apply to your project. Include existing permanent trees, large shrubs, vines, and lawn, since these are rarely moved.

Step 2—Drawing the Base Plan

When all the measuring is completed you have a field sketch that records with dimensions the size and place of everything in your yard, but it isn't a plan. A plan transforms your sketch and dimensions into a scaled "map" of your property from which you can measure accurately. There are two common scales for home plans: $\frac{1}{4}'' = 1'$ and $\frac{1}{8}'' = 1'$. Even if you don't have any drawing or drafting experience, drawing a plan to scale isn't difficult. Most office- or drafting-supply stores will have the four items listed below (but don't fall for all the other fun drafting equipment while shopping because you won't need it):

1. **Paper for the plan—vellum.** Vellum is a semitransparent drafting paper that erases cleanly time after time. You need to use vellum to make blueprints of plans too large for a photocopy machine. Vellum is sold in precut sheets in many sizes. It's also available preprinted with a bright blue grid that doesn't show up in the blueprint process but which does reproduce on a copy machine. If you buy

vellum with a grid the same size as the scale you're using, you are assured a more accurate drawing using fewer drafting tools.

The following list tells you how large an image you may draw on each sheet size at the two most common scales: ⅛" = 1' and ¼" = 1'.

Sheet Size	Margins	Scale	Maximum Image Size
24" × 36"	2" each side	⅛"	160' × 256'
24" × 36"	2"	¼"	80' × 128'
11" × 17"	1"	⅛"	72' × 120'
11" × 17"	1"	¼"	36' × 60'
8½" × 11"	½"	⅛"	60' × 80'
8½" × 11"	½"	¼"	30' × 40'

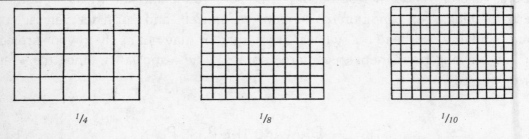

Examples of grids to scale: ¼ inch = 1 foot for small spaces, ⅛ inch = 1 foot for regular house on a lot, 1 inch = 10 feet for large suburban or rural sites.

2. **An architect's scale.** A standard ruler shows each inch divided into 8 or 16 equal parts by short lines marking each increment. To work at a scale of 8 feet to the inch (a popular scale), you would have to count each ⅛" increment for every foot of measurement. It is difficult and time-consuming to transpose these increments into a working scale from a ruler because they are so small, and the chances of error would increase with each calculation you make.

To solve this problem, the architect's scale was devised. This is a foot-long ruler that is divided by lines into increments numbered consecutively from 1 to approximately 92. The architect's scale usually provides for two different working scales: the most common, ⅛" = 1'; and for very small projects, ¼" = 1'. For extremely large plans, architects use an engineer's scale, which is divided into a scale of 1" = 10'.

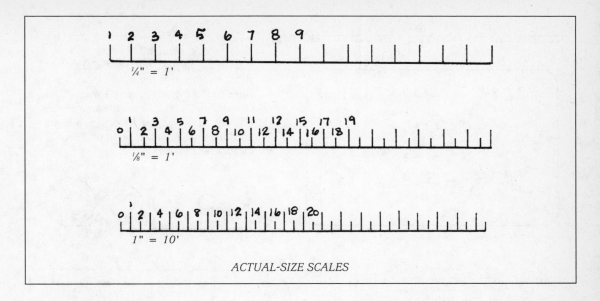

ACTUAL-SIZE SCALES

3. **A soft lead pencil and eraser.** Soft lead is designated as #2, #1, F, or HB. When drawing on vellum, a soft lead ensures that you can draw bold lines without leaving a big groove in the paper that may not erase well. Virtually any pencil with soft lead will do, but be sure it is well sharpened. (Don't worry if you get a lot of smudging from the pencil on your plan; this is a working plan, not a show plan, and its function is strictly to convey information.) A good eraser is also important in creating your plan. If you've ever seen how erasers dry up on older pencils, you know it's well worth the fifty cents for a new one, and I recommend Pentel Clic erasers.

4. **The all-purpose template.** Here's another cheap but essential tool of the drafter's trade. I recommend you buy one that has a series of smaller circles plus a similar series of rectilinear shapes such as squares and rectangles. You'll use this inexpensive little tool to draw to scale on your plan such circular objects as pots, tree trunks, fountains, outdoor tables, and all sorts of curving objects. The squares come in handy for drawing in outdoor furniture, precast stepping-stones, troughs, and square pots exactly to scale. If you need to draw circles too large for the template use a cheap student pencil compass.

A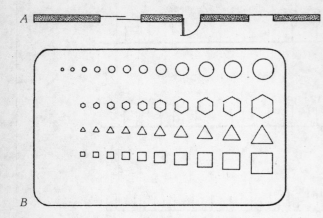

B

A. This example shows how to draw the house walls, windows, and doors. B. A typical all-purpose template. C. Examples of actual-size template circles applied to the scale ⅛ inch = 1 foot. A diameter of ⅛ inch here indicates a plant of 1-foot diameter on your plan, a diameter of ¼ inch equals a plant of 2-foot diameter, and so on.

C

Now that you have your drafting tools and the field sketch before you on the table, it is time to transfer the numerical data onto the vellum sheet. Position the property lines on the vellum so that they are centered, with a comfortable margin around the edges. Then transfer the footprint of the house by drawing walls, then doors and windows. Finally, add the rest of the items on the field sketch to the vellum plan. When all is drawn to scale, you have an accurate base plan from which to work.

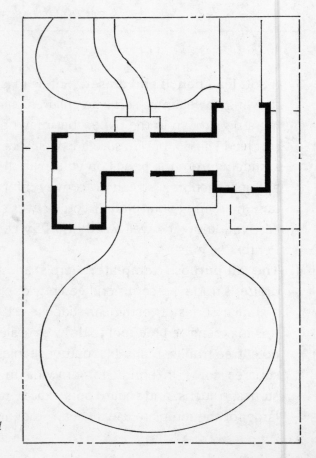

Base Plan   This drawing shows base plan information including fences, edges of the lawn, driveway, entry walk and stoop, back patio, and utility yard.

STEP 3—IDENTIFY PLANTING ZONES

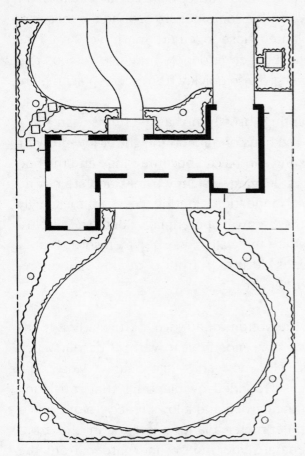

Since plants are the least expensive and most brilliant part of a landscape makeover, it helps to identify on your plan where they fit into your garden. The locations discussed below identify the spaces where plants may be grown. Once all the possible planting areas are outlined on your plan, move on to the next step.

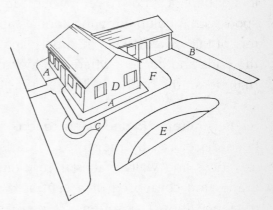

Planting Zones   Existing trees to remain are shown by circles on this plan; squiggly lines define all the places that need new planting.

Places for Plants   Most of the planting you do falls into one of six basic categories illustrated in this diagram. If you keep this in mind you'll be more sure of plant selection and will enjoy a more successful garden in the long run. A. foundation, B. perimeter, C. edges, D. vertical, E. massing, F. containers.

Foundations: Foundation planting is a term used to describe the planting around the base of a house that covers up the vents, exposed footings, and utilities. Most but not all homes have existing evergreens and hardy shrubs around the foundations. Foundation planting concepts also apply to the edges of decks to disguise the supports if there is no siding.

Where foundation planting is absent, you can rely on big bushy plants from our lists for coverage in one season. Marguerites and euryops daisies are ideal since growers offer them in the much larger five-gallon container sizes, although these are expensive. But they do the job well if planted close together, and in very mild climates they may become semipermanent. Budget gardeners may use cosmos and giant zinnias in the sunny spots; since they grow so quickly from seed you can plant an entire wall for pennies.

Homes with existing foundation planting, usually of hardy shrubs, can often benefit from the addition at the front of the beds of medium-height or low-growing plants. This is because over time the existing shrubs can become rangy and the bottom branches may die out for lack of light, leaving unsightly trunks and stems and lots of bare ground. To renew such an old foundation planting, cover up these ugly spots with medium-growing annuals and fast-growing perennials. Spot in a few clusters of tall spike flowers in larger gaps where the wall shows between shrubs, or at the ends and corners where the look needs closure. In front of all these fill the remainder of the bed with short stuff as borders or masses.

Perimeter: No one wants to look at the bottom of a fence, particularly if it has been discolored by moisture, and a lawn that ends next to vertical barriers such as fences and walls makes it very difficult to mow and edge cleanly. Most landscapes are composed of a central lawn surrounded by plantings that run along the fence lines. This softens the edges of the garden and allows fences to disappear behind mounding plants and flowers. Perimeter planting occurs in the front yard, too, where it helps to visually separate your house and garden from the neighbor's.

The key to beautiful perimeters is realizing that plants at the far back of the yard need to be larger than elsewhere in the garden. This is because small plants may get lost at that distance. But even if you use big plants, be sure to use lots of them to ensure the visual effect is bold enough. For example, a cosmos grows large, but its flowers are not particularly dense and they sit upon wiry stems at the top. Just one cosmos may not generate enough color impact at the rear of a big yard, so be sure to use a bunch of them planted closely together for a clearly visible mass. Plants from our lists designated as small literally disappear with distance, so be sure to compensate by using medium, tall, or bushy plants in increased quantities further out.

Islands: Some gardeners break up expanses of lawn with islands of flowers and perhaps a small accent tree or shrub. Islands increase your flower-gardening area and add interest to an otherwise dull lawn. Inexperienced gardeners tend to make these perfectly round, which projects a very formal look that sometimes fails to complement the rest of the landscaping style. Your islands may take any shape you wish. Combining two or more in creative natural forms makes the green lawn drift in and around them, like the ocean separating rocky outcroppings along a shoreline. Use low-growing plants around the edges of the island, then medium-size flowers, and finally tall spikes at the center, with their brilliant spires towering over the rest. You could replace spikes with a specimen shrub or tree depending on your taste and budget.

Edgings: When you add a creative edging of plants, you transform that space from a dull feature to one that is highlighted with color. And you may add edging to practically anything, be it a sidewalk, flagstone path, patio, or fence line. Edging with plants creates more than just a boundary; it enhances the space with bands of one or more flower colors. A simple sidewalk bound by lawn becomes a yellow-brick road when you cut out strips of turf and replace it with edges of dwarf marigolds. If there is nothing in place to edge with flowers, add a simple set of concrete stepping-stones. It need not have a destination, and may end at a birdbath, sundial, or simple fountain.

In the old days shrub hedges weren't planted in a single row of plants, but in two parallel but offset rows. If a shrub died, there would be others very close by to fill the gap quickly. Since shrubs grow slowly, the loss of a shrub in a single-row hedge leaves a sizable gap until replanted, and then it takes even more time to mature and make the hedge continuous once again. The key to edging success using our quick-fix plants is to arrange them very close together so that the effect is continuous. Novice gardeners often make the mistake of planting too sparsely so that when completed the effect barely suggests edging. Using a double offset row not only ensures that a few dead plants don't ruin the effect, but that the flower color will appear more dense. An edging also looks much better if planted in a single flower color rather than a mixture.

Vertical gardening: Most people tend to see their garden plan in just one dimension: the ground plane. But there is a second dimension that is a wonderful problem solver for small spaces and which lends more character to planting. The vertical plane occurs along walls and fences, upon support posts or columns, and overhead in arbors and shade structures. Thanks to new options in container gardening, vertical planting can be done just about anywhere there is a vertical to support plants. You'll find specifics on container gardens in chapter 4.

To really take advantage of vertical gardening, refer to the fast-growing vines in our plant palette (see chapter 3). They may be grown strictly for their foliage or flowers, depending on your needs and climate. For example, bottle gourds are ideal fast foliage makers and will grow to thirty feet or more in just a month or two, and their large leaves really cast a lot of shade.

The Victorian gardener knew of the value of such plants and considered a gazebo or arbor much more attractive when shrouded in morning glory or trumpet

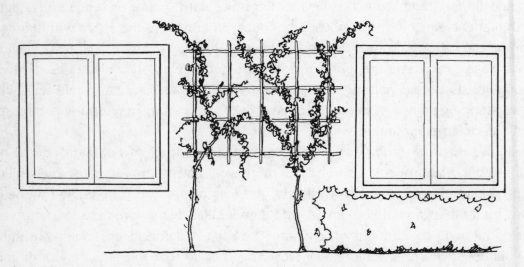

Vertical Gardening   The main element that gives country or cottage gardens their casual charm is the generous use of vines and vinelike plants draped over windows and trained onto otherwise unattractive or dull walls. Don't be afraid of vines damaging your walls if you use a trellis like the one shown here to support the vine runners.

vines. Our great-grandmothers beautified their homesteads with annual vines by covering everything from well houses to chicken coops in living foliage. This shows what great opportunities vertical gardening offers in terms of cover-ups.

Wherever you have a wall, there is an opportunity for vertical gardening—an especially effective way to create landscapes in the city. Consider the exposure of any features such as windows or doorways. You can plant a fast-growing vine beside such openings, in the ground or a container, and train the leafy runners up one side and over the top if you have a sufficiently long season. Gourd vines, for example, grow very quickly on south- or west-facing walls where there is lots of heat, and in a period of just six weeks they can completely transform a common back door into an inviting entry.

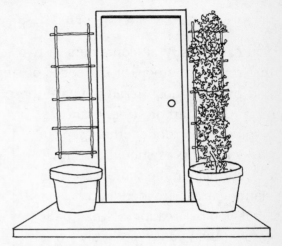

What was once just a plain back door becomes gardenesque through container gardening. A fast-growing vine planted in a big pot will snake its way up the little stick-ladder trellis attached to the wall beside the door. Eventually the vine on each side will meet at the top, creating a full arch of greenery.

To beautify dull blank walls use a lightweight trellis and attach it where you want the vine to grow. You can buy either a prefabricated grid or fan-shaped trellis at the home improvement store or make one yourself out of sticks for free. Salvage limbs that are long and straight from tree trimmers, or harvest them from your own pruning projects. Cut off all the lateral sprouts from the limb and strip off the leaves. Lay out the sticks in a grid or ladder shape on the ground, then connect the pieces using tie wire or wood screws as tightly as you can. Mount the finished trellis on the wall and start training your annual vines. It is exciting to work with these fast-growing plants since they are guaranteed to be rewarding the very first season.

If you frequent garage sales or junk yards, you may find other containers to use as part of your vertical gardening scheme. That old rusting wrought iron bookshelf that went out with the 1970s, for example, may be just the thing to add pizzazz to blank walls, particularly where space is limited, like side yards and entryways. To resurrect one of these into an attractive plant shelf, simply sand away the rust and repaint in white, black, or hunter green. Even if it starts rusting again, it will add charm when covered with luscious, container-grown foliage and flowers.

STEP 4—SHOW CONTAINERS

You can classify all containers in two ways. *Terrestrial* pots are arranged around the front door stoop, at the edges of steps, driveway corners, and on wood decks and paved patios. *Aerial* pots are those that hang from overhead structures such as a shade arbor, tree branches, awnings, and roof overhangs. Your baskets and pots should be shown on your plan in the same way other planting areas are identified.

If you're creating a small patio garden, then you're probably working at a scale of ¼ inch = 1 foot. At this scale you can draw each container on your plan so the exact shape and size are clearly visible. Use

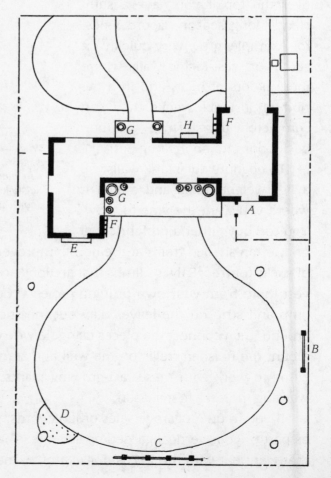

*Containers and Vertical Gardening Plan
This diagram shows where container plants are to be located and where you'll need a drip system to water them. Drawing in each pot allows you to more accurately estimate how many plants you must buy to fill them all. Also shown here are a variety of inexpensive ideas for vertical gardening and containers: A. twig arch over gateway to utility yard. B. freestanding background screen. C. post and beam arbor. D. new paving—bricks laid on sand bed. E. shelf for pots or a window box. F. grid arbor attached to bare house wall. G. color pots. H. faux window with shelf or window box beneath.*

the circle template to draw each pot exactly where you wish it to be, and later you can assign plants to each one. If you're using containers in the context of an entire backyard garden drawn at $\frac{1}{8}$ inch = 1 foot, a 6-inch-diameter pot will be too small to read well. An option is to draw all pots in the same way, then assign a number to each which corresponds to a separate list bearing the dimensions. For example, pots 1, 2, and 3 are all 12 inches in diameter; pots 4 and 5 are 18 inches, and so on.

Remember that pots and hanging baskets need a water source, be it sprinklers, a drip system, or your garden hose. If it's difficult to water certain pots or baskets, they may end up languishing for lack of care. If you have persistent wind problems, be careful where you plan hanging baskets. Since the potting soil is held by little more than packed moss, wind can reach down and dehydrate the root zone far faster than in pots. Wind can also make hanging plants of all kinds swing, something some people find aggravating.

Hanging baskets can be placed wherever they are most attractive and out of the way of traffic. Consider the strength of the rafter from which the pot or basket will hang; some just aren't strong enough for one large container or the combined weight of many smaller ones. Also keep in mind that hanging baskets and most hanging pots lack drip pans, so the paving, planting, or furniture beneath is vulnerable to the effects of continuous drainage. For drought-conscious gardeners, placing hanging baskets over ground planters or other pots uses the drainage from the hanging basket to water a second time.

Half moss baskets planted with flowers or long vines such as dwarf ivies (both green and variegated) or jasmine are another way you can use containers to liven up a dull wall space. Do keep in mind that flush-mounted half baskets can cause some discoloration of the wall both behind the basket itself and below, where drainage may support algae or mildew. You may want to consider moving them from time to time.

If you have posts or supports for awnings but no nearby planting area, use containers to support vine plants. Simply wrap some tie wire around the posts all the way up to the top, and use bread or garbage bag ties to attach vine runners as they grow. This transforms an ugly steel post into a leafy colonnade. Once the vine reaches the roof beam, train it horizontally to take greatest advantage of every runner it puts out. Perhaps later on when long-term planting replaces these first-season dazzlers, the new vine can use the very same support system.

If there's a window on the wall, even if it doesn't open, consider a window box or a series of them just below the sill. They will make the window much more attractive, not only from the outside but from the inside as well. Purchase sturdy metal shelving brackets and mount them on the wall just below the window. Use a redwood board painted or stained to match the house or steel mesh to create the shelf. The mesh should be heavy; try the $\frac{1}{8}$-inch-gauge graduated mesh panels used for security and be sure to prime and paint them to reduce rust. Mesh is better for drainage than a solid shelf, particularly where there is snow, and will hold up a lot longer.

There are two ways to achieve the charming window-box effect. You can consider a simple shelf using wood or metal supports that you can find at any hardware store, or you can install an official window box or shell to contain one. Line up your flower pots for a beautiful view both indoors and out.

Using a shelf allows you more options than attaching a box to the sill. You can set a traditional window box upon it, or arrange a quaint row of terra-cotta flower pots filled with blooming annuals, bulbs, or herbs.

Do keep in mind that you don't need a real window to create this effect. An old wooden window hung on the wall or a pair of brightly painted shutters hung in a closed position provides the same effect, making a suitable background for window boxes or other container combinations. Paint the back side of the window panes before hanging so you don't see the building wall through them. If it's a single-pane window, consider replacing it with a mirror to give the illusion of yet another room beyond.

STEP 5—COLOR ON THE CANVAS

Your plan should now show you exactly where there is space for planting. These spaces represent a blank canvas upon which you may apply color. The scheme you choose is purely a personal choice, but there may be special factors which govern your decisions. Most people like all flower colors, but some people prefer cool colors, or any but white, or have other similar preferences. And if you are planting for a special event such as a wedding with a color theme, then flower color is more important and should be carefully chosen.

Most colors can be classified as either warm or cool. Warm colors include red, magenta, orange, and canary-yellow, all of which are very bold and powerful. They are exciting to look at and lend a festive character to plantings. Cool colors, on the other hand, include the spectrum of blues, violet, white, soft pink, and palest yellow. White, yellow, and pale pink are the last to disappear at dusk because they magnify or reflect the dim light, while other colors absorb it.

Light colors have a great ability to magnify sunlight, which is lovely in the evening, but can increase glare in bright areas at noon on a summer day. Green is also classified as a cool color, but since it rarely occurs in flowers it is treated as a neutral background for both warm- and cool-colored flowers.

It is interesting to note how economics affects the popularity of certain colors. When money is tight, people seek more bang for their buck by using potent but traditional schemes. According to color expert Ken Charbonneau, who was enlisted by the National Garden Bureau to explain color trends, purple and violet are now favored over blues, peach has given way to coral, pink to magenta, and red to burgundy.

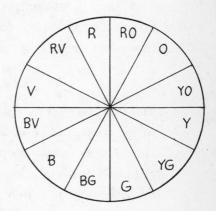

To really understand how color works, buy a paper color wheel from the art supply store or use the example shown here. It includes all the basic hues and shows how they relate to one another. Clockwise around the color wheel you'll find that

If you don't have a color wheel, use this one to see how the colors are arranged. All color wheels resemble this one whether printed in color or described in a diagram.

blue blends into violet, then into red, followed by orange, yellow, green, and back to blue again. When you arrange colors in this way they naturally flow into one another. If you arrange them out of order they exhibit much greater contrast. When you combine complementary colors, or those located opposite from one another on the color wheel, a unique scenario occurs. The human eye senses a certain vibration between complementary colors when placed side by side that can be uncomfortable or exciting to look at, and which adds to the visual dynamics of a garden.

The best-known use of these complementary hues are the Christmas colors, red and green. They create lots of excitement during the holidays when there are few other colors in the winter landscape, and this vibration is lovely against the emptiness of white snow. But we rarely combine them in clothing (except plaids) because the vibration visually conflicts with the person wearing the clothes. Yellow and violet are also opposites and can be quite beautiful in the Johnny-jump-up viola flower.

These differences are important to interior decorators, because in order for the garden to become an extension of the indoors, the two must flow together. This is of greater importance if there are large picture windows and sliding glass doors opening onto the garden. Imagine a beautiful English country interior with soft pink, lavender, and white floral patterns combined with vivid green fabrics and carpet. If the garden outside was planted in blood-red hollyhocks, gold African marigolds, and coral roses, there would be a great contrast obvious even to the untrained eye. Despite the fact that the observer may not perceive the difference, they would find the scheme much more dramatic if the indoor and outdoor spaces all projected an integrated scheme.

Tightwad Gardening Tip: Avoid using too many shades of the same color in one area, and consider colors of surrounding hardscape elements as well. For example, deep red geraniums or red salvia planted against a red brick wall or beside red clay pavers does not offer us much contrast or visual appeal. When such similar colors are used together they tend to make each other appear overly bright or muddy in comparison. Contrast is the key to making each color spot boldly effective, and guarantees maximum visual impact from each plant you buy.

It's a good idea to buy yourself a cheap set of colored pencils before selecting colors. The pencils are erasable and can be used to experiment with color on a copy of your plan. If you already know your color scheme, whether it is warm or cool, pull out pencils of those shades and leave the rest in the box. Should you be less picky, pull out all the basics like red, orange, yellow, purple, pink, and blue. If you are coloring for a straight makeover, you need not be so exacting in terms of season. But if you are planning toward a specific event, stay loose and flexible about color, because each one you use must be matched with a flower that blooms in that range of hue and produces during the right part of the season.

Take into consideration what you see from each window of the house if you are attempting to match an interior color scheme. These are the places where your gardening effort will be most visible and appreciated. This is a lot like a color-by-numbers set, except that you get to decide what color to use, where the color is to go, and how large it will be. For example, don't just fill a planting space with one mass of color; use a strip of edging color against the lawn, and background color along the fence line.

Work your way through the entire plan with your colored pencils. Be thorough and try to visualize each and every planter or pot planted and blooming before you make a final decision. If you don't visualize well it takes much longer. Anyone with artistic ability or those in design-related professions will be a big help with color selection. If you

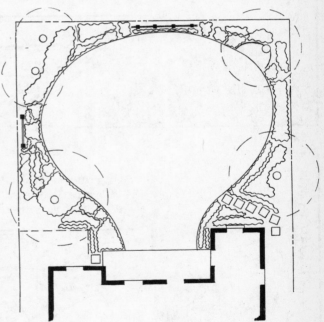

Color Zones   The same backyard shown in the overall plans is blown up here to give you a better sense of how color zones work. We are still working within the limits of the planting zones, but now they are split up into smaller areas. Use your colored pencils to shade each color zone. To experiment with various schemes, lay a piece of tracing paper on top and try different combinations before you settle on the best one.

later have problems applying plants to the colors, feel free to make changes as needed.

All of the recommended fast-growing bedding plants profiled in the plant palette in chapter 3 are reclassified below in Bloom Color Lists to give you a quick reference when matching colors to plants. If you have chosen a certain place to grow blue flowers, simply run down the list of blues to get an overview of what varieties rep-

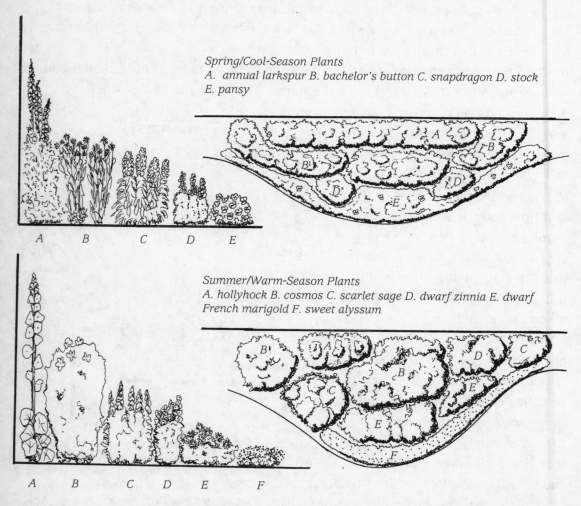

Spring/Cool-Season Plants
A. annual larkspur B. bachelor's button C. snapdragon D. stock
E. pansy

Summer/Warm-Season Plants
A. hollyhock B. cosmos C. scarlet sage D. dwarf zinnia E. dwarf
French marigold F. sweet alyssum

The two diagrams at left, above, show you how plant heights are arranged to allow each plant to receive maximum sunlight and visibility. They are also shown from above, at right, to give you a better sense of groups, edging, and masses.

resent the color. Some plants like pansies and petunias are available in nearly every color of the rainbow, so these will pop up in most of the color categories. This is also a sign that the plant is popular enough to have been bred into an abundance of cultivars, further attesting to its versatility and ease of cultivation.

Height has also been added to the Bloom Color Lists to allow you to see instantly which plants are short enough to grow in front and which are tall and strictly for the rear. Placing taller plants to the rear not only allows you to see every plant, but also ensures that all receive equal amounts of sunlight. The height designations also help you to know which plants are more suited to containers and hanging baskets. The exact number of plants is not part of this chart and will be covered in chapter 6 as part of the estimating process.

BLOOM COLOR LISTS

Abbreviations: B = big and bushy T = tall spike M = medium S = short V = vines H = hanging plant
(Chapter 3 has information on climate criteria.)

Plants That Bloom in Red, Brick-Red, Brown, and Magenta

Name	Height	Exposure	Type
Anemone	S	Sun	Bulb
Begonia, wax	S	Shade	Annual
Cineraria	S	Shade	Annual
Cosmos	B	Sun	Annual
Dahlia, bedding	M	Part sun	Annual
Fuchsia	H	Shade	Perennial
Geranium	M/V	Sun	Annual
Gladiolus	T	Sun	Bulb
Hollyhock	T	Sun	Biennial
Impatiens	S	Shade	Annual
Marigold, French	S	Sun	Annual
Pansy	S	Variable	Annual
Petunia	S	Sun	Annual
Primrose	S	Shade	Annual
Ranunculus	S	Sun	Bulb
Rudbeckia	B	Sun	Perennial
Scarlet runner bean	V	Sun	Annual
Scarlet sage	M	Sun	Annual
Snapdragon	M/S	Sun	Annual

Name	Height	Exposure	Type
Sweet pea	V	Sun	Annual
Tulip	M/S	Sun	Bulb
Verbena	V	Sun	Perennial
Zinnia	B/S	Sun	Annual

Plants That Bloom in Purple or Violet

Name	Height	Exposure	Type
Anemone	S	Sun	Bulb
Aubretia	S	Variable	Perennial
Cineraria	S	Shade	Annual
Columbine	M	Part sun	Biennial
Dahlia, bedding	M	Part sun	Annual
Foxglove	S	Shade	Biennial
Fuchsia	H	Shade	Perennial
Hollyhock	S	Sun	Biennial
Johnny-jump-up	S	Variable	Annual
Morning glory	V	Sun	Annual
Pansy	S	Variable	Annual
Periwinkle	S	Part sun	Annual
Petunia	S	Sun	Annual
Snapdragon	M/S	Sun	Annual
Stock	M	Part sun	Annual
Sweet alyssum	S	Sun	Annual
Sweet pea	V	Sun	Annual
Verbena	V	Sun	Perennial
Viola	S	Variable	Annual

Plants That Bloom in Blue, Ultramarine, and Azure

Name	Height	Exposure	Type
Ageratum	S	Sun	Annual
Bachelor's button	M	Sun	Annual
Blue salvia	M	Part sun	Annual
Cineraria	S	Shade	Annual
Delphinium	T	Part sun	Perennial
Larkspur	T	Sun	Annual
Lobelia	S	Sun	Annual
Pansy	S	Variable	Annual
Petunia	S	Sun	Annual
Primrose	S	Shade	Annual
Viola	S	Variable	Annual

Plants That Bloom in Yellow and Gold

Name	Height	Exposure	Type
Anemone	S	Sun	Bulb
Begonia, tuberous	H	Shade	Bulb
Calendula	M/S	Sun	Annual
California poppy	S	Sun	Annual
Columbine	M	Part sun	Biennial
Daffodil	S	Sun	Bulb
Dahlia, bedding	M	Part sun	Annual
Daisy, Euryops	B	Sun	Perennial
Dusty miller	M	Sun	Annual
Gladiolus	T	Sun	Bulb
Hollyhock	T	Sun	Biennial
Marigold	M/S	Sun	Annual
Nasturtium	V/H	Sun	Annual
Pansy	S	Variable	Annual
Primrose	S	Shade	Annual
Ranunculus	S	Sun	Bulb
Rudbeckia	B	Sun	Perennial
Snapdragon	M/S	Sun	Annual
Sunflower	T/B	Sun	Annual
Sweet pea	V	Sun	Annual
Tulip	M/S	Sun	Bulb
Viola	S	Variable	Annual
Zinnia	B/S	Sun	Annual

Plants That Bloom in Orange

Name	Height	Exposure	Type
Anemone	S	Sun	Bulb
Begonia, tuberous	H	Shade	Bulb
Calendula	M/S	Sun	Annual
Dahlia, bedding	S	Part sun	Annual
Geranium	M/V	Sun	Annual
Gladiolus	T	Sun	Bulb
Marigold	M/S	Sun	Annual
Nasturtium	V/H	Variable	Annual
Ranunculus	S	Sun	Bulb
Rudbeckia	B	Sun	Perennial
Snapdragon	M/S	Sun	Annual
Sweet pea	V	Sun	Annual
Tulip	M/S	Sun	Bulb
Viola	S	Variable	Annual
Zinnia	B/S	Sun	Annual

Plants That Bloom in Pink, Magenta, and Mauve

Name	Height	Exposure	Type
Aubretia	S	Variable	Perennial
Bachelor's button	M	Sun	Annual
Begonia, wax	S	Shade	Annual
Columbine	M	Variable	Biennial
Dahlia, bedding	S	Part sun	Annual
Foxglove	T	Shade	Biennial
Fuchsia	H	Shade	Perennial
Geranium	M/V	Sun	Annual
Gladiolus	T	Sun	Bulb
Hollyhock	T	Sun	Biennial
Impatiens	S	Shade	Annual
Larkspur	T	Sun	Annual
Marguerite	B	Sun	Perennial
Periwinkle	S	Variable	Annual
Petunia	S	Sun	Annual
Snapdragon	M/S	Sun	Annual
Stock	M	Sun	Annual
Sweet pea	V	Sun	Annual
Tulip	S/M	Sun	Bulb
Zinnia	B/S	Sun	Annual

Plants That Bloom in White, Beige, and Cream

Name	Height	Exposure	Type
Begonia, wax	S	Shade	Annual
Daffodil	S	Sun	Bulb
Foxglove	T	Shade	Biennial
Geranium	M/V	Sun	Annual
Gladiolus	T	Sun	Bulb
Gourd, bottle	V	Sun	Annual
Impatiens	S	Shade	Annual
Marguerite	B	Sun	Perennial
Morning glory	V	Sun	Annual
Periwinkle	S	Variable	Annual
Petunia	S	Sun	Annual
Snapdragon	M/S	Sun	Annual
Stock	M	Sun	Annual
Sweet alyssum	S	Sun	Annual
Sweet pea	V	Sun	Annual

STEP 6—CHOOSE PLANTS

It helps to visualize how you want each planting area to look, but if you aren't imaginative, the step-by-step approach detailed below ensures you'll end up with a lovely garden anyway. The key is using the Bloom Color Lists exactly as instructed.

It's best to start this step at one side of the plan and work your way through one area at a time. Don't jump around because this causes you to lose the continuity you need to get through the process smoothly. Use a two- or three-letter abbreviation in the margin or beside a color zone to reference a plant. You may also write a number beside each plant in the lists above, then write it on the plan to reference the plant as you work through the garden. A systematic approach and thoroughness are the keys to success. Here is an example of how to approach each planting area.

a. Choose a planter and note its exposure. Let's say it receives full sun.

b. Note the different color zones you've chosen. Let's say there are five: a yellow border in front, two zones of white and blue in the middle, and two larger zones to the rear that are red and pink.

c. Start with the yellow color zone at the front because the shortest plants must always be located there. Go to the lists and choose a plant that blooms in

Cataloging Exposures   Here the exposures of each planting zone have been cataloged with abbreviations. SH means predominantly shady, PS is partially shady most of the day due to tree canopy or building shadows, AS indicates afternoon sun, which will be very hot in the summertime, MS is morning sun—ideal for many plants that can't take the heat, and S is where the planting gets even, full sunlight for most of the day.

that color, takes full sun, and is short. For our example, let's choose yellow dwarf French marigolds. Use a pencil to mark an abbreviation for this plant in the yellow zone. You can erase this later on.

    d. Move to the middle plants—the white and blue zones. Consult the lists once again for these colors in medium-sized plants that take full sun. We'll choose white zonal geraniums and blue salvia. Write the abbreviations on these color zones as well.

    e. Move to the rear plants—the red and pink zones. Scan the lists for color and for tall or bushy plants designated for full sun. We'll use tall red gladiolus and bushy pink cosmos.

STEP 7—ASSIGN PLANTS TO CONTAINERS

Before you begin choosing plants for your containers, visit a local retail garden center to inspect their already planted pots and baskets. There you'll see how different flowers look together and how their growth habits compare. Garden centers use foolproof combinations of flowers, which make ideal guidelines for your own containers.

    Bring your measuring tape and paper tablet to record the diameters of pots and baskets at the nursery, then count how many plants are growing in a typical large, medium, and small pot or basket. This gives you a rough guideline to work with when you sit down to estimate how many plants, pots, and supplies you can afford. While at the garden center, record the prices of the empty pots, wire baskets, sphagnum moss, and potting soil so you can compare them against prices elsewhere.

    The simplest way to assign plants to your containers is to create a typical example of the three sized containers discussed above. Using a standard is less confusing and allows you to organize them, which in turn makes the cost estimate and shopping far easier.

    There is a great deal of freedom when it comes to choosing what to grow in containers, but for best success, consider these three fundamental requirements when making your decisions.

    1. **Exposure:** Each pot or basket is a miniature flower bed, and like any part of the landscape it is assigned a particular solar exposure, such as full sun, part sun, shade, or part shade. These are determined not by the pot itself but by *the exposure of the place where it is to sit.* If you move the pot, most likely you'll change the exposure.

This shows how important it is to know where your pots will be so they can be planted to suit the exposure of that location. All the plants in a particular pot must share the same exposure preference if they are to grow and bloom successfully together.

2. **Form:** The size, shape, and growth habit of the plants you select are important. Plants suited to pots and those for hanging baskets have specific forms that determine how they are used. The two best forms for container gardens are compact or cascading.

Compact plants are used in the center of a pot or basket to fill it with flowers. They can be natural in size or dwarf forms of larger flowering annuals. Good examples of naturals for this purpose are wax begonias, pansies, impatiens, and marigolds; calendula and zinnia are dwarf forms of larger annuals.

Cascading plants are set at the edges of the pot, or planted in the walls of a hanging basket so they can drip down the sides. The best flowering examples of cascading plants are lobelia, sweet alyssum, Johnny-jump-ups, and ivy geraniums. Extralong cascading plants are restricted to hanging pots or baskets so that the tresses can drape into an almost columnar form when mature. Examples of these include nasturtium, ivy geraniums, and morning glory, but you can also take advantage of foliage plants such as variegated dwarf periwinkle and the huge assortment of miniature ivies. Some specialty plants like fuchsias are rarely mixed with other plants because they are a bit more finicky and large enough to stand on their own.

3. **Color:** Growing container gardens is more fun than traditional flower beds because they are planted in a riot of colors like living confetti. Since a multitude of pots can be ganged together or rearranged, you have much more flexibility than when planting in the ground. It is this unbridled expression of color that makes it easy for the novice to create stunning displays in hanging baskets and pots with a cornucopia of different plants.

The palette of plants available in California is mind-boggling compared to that of New York. That's why gardening in mild climates is so free, but often overwhelming with so many choices to make. Should you feel confused, try choosing a limited palette and working strictly from a handful of plants you know best. Some of the most common combinations are grouped here by exposure so you won't have to look them up each time. They are well tested and guaranteed to give you an eye-popping, vigorous display.

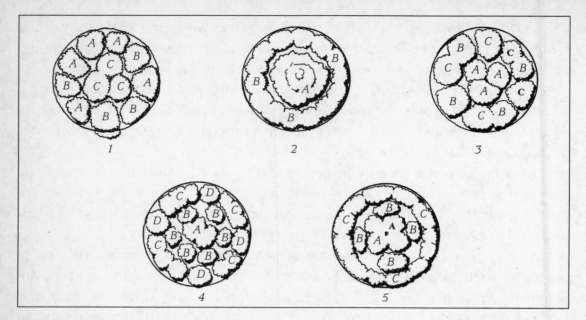

Winning Container Combinations
1. *Sun pot I — A. sweet alyssum B. blue lobelia C. dwarf French marigold*
2. *Sun pot II— A. dusty miller B. mixed petunias*
3. *Sun pot III — A. scarlet sage B. dwarf French marigold C. ivy geranium*
4. *Spring/Cool-Season pot — A. Johnny-jump-up B. stock or dwarf snapdragon*
                            C. English primrose D. anemone
5. *Shade pot — A. wax begonia B. cineraria C. impatiens*

WINNING CONTAINER PLANT COMBINATIONS BY EXPOSURE

Compatible Plants for Shaded Areas

Name	Form	Colors
Begonia, wax	Upright	Pink, Red, White
Cineraria	Upright	Multicolor
Impatiens	Upright	Pink, Orange, White
Ivy geranium	Cascading	Pink, Red, White
Lobelia	Cascading	Shades of Blue
Periwinkle	Upright	White, Pink
Primrose	Upright	Multicolor
Sweet alyssum	Cascading	White, Purple
Viola	Semiupright	Multicolor

Compatible Plants for Full Sun

Name	Form	Colors
Dwarf African marigold	Upright	Yellow, Orange
Dwarf French marigold	Upright	Yellow, Orange, Red
Dwarf zinnia	Upright	Multicolor
Geranium, zonal	Upright	Red, Pink, Orange, White
Ivy geranium	Cascading	Pink, Red, Orange, White
Marguerite	Upright Bushy	White, Pink
Nasturtium	Cascading	Red, Yellow, Orange
Petunia	Semicascading	Multicolor
Red salvia	Upright	Red, Blue
Sweet alyssum	Cascading	White, Purple

Compatible Plants for Cool Season—Variable Exposure

Name	Form	Colors
Ageratum	Upright	Blue
Anemone	Upright	Multicolor
Dahlia, bedding	Upright	Multicolor
Dwarf snapdragon	Upright	Multicolor
Lobelia	Cascading	Blue
Nasturtium	Cascading	Red, Orange, Yellow
Pansy	Upright	Multicolor
Periwinkle	Upright	White, Violet
Primrose	Upright	Multicolor
Sweet alyssum	Cascading	White, Purple
Viola	Semicascading	Multicolor

Useful and beautiful: One of the fundamental goals of budget gardening is to get the very most out of your garden. If you can plant herb or food plants in your pots of flowers, you enjoy more than just beautiful color. The plants are close at hand for nipping off a bit of seasoning or garnish that turns dinner into a dining experience. So many gardeners have discovered these useful plant options that nurseries frequently include parsley, chives, chamomile, and basil in their color bedding plant displays.

There are specific combinations you can use that ensure all your food plants share similar solar exposures. Whether you are planting for zesty salads, fresh culinary herbs, edible flowers, or just a handful of medicinals for healing teas, they must all thrive to become attractive plants. Your containers are not just a source of useful

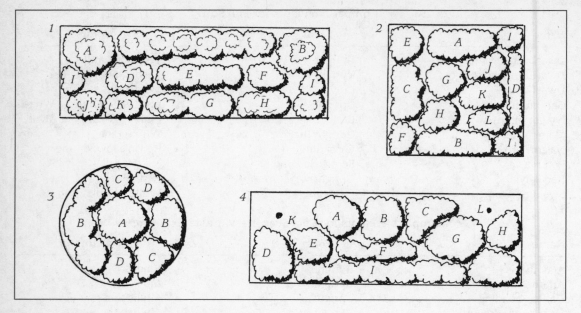

Winning Kitchen Garden Combinations
1. Nouvelle Cuisine Window Box or Trough Garden — A. patio tomato B. pepper C. leaf lettuce D. parsley
　　E. chives F. coriander (cilantro) G. nasturtium H. kale I. basil
2. Easy-to-Grow Herb Garden — A. sage B. thyme C. oregano D. chives E. basil F. rosemary G. mint
　　H. parsley I. coriander (cilantro) J. Italian parsley K. calendula L. lavender
3. Edible Flower/Garnish Pot — A. dwarf calendula B. viola C. nasturtium D. Johnny-jump-up
4. Medicinal Health Herb Trough or Window Box — A. feverfew B. comfrey C. garlic D. verbena
　　E. lemon balm F. chamomile G. peppermint H. yarrow I. viola J. rosemary

plants, they must double as a beautiful part of the garden as well. (For more information on food plants in the palette turn to chapter 3.)

　　As you work through the planting areas, all sorts of ideas, relationships, and conclusions will run through your head. Unless you jot down the ideas, they may vanish altogether. It's fine to make little notes all over your working plan—in the margins and empty spaces—to remind you later on. Remember, this is not a work of art but a diagram designed to communicate ideas. Nothing at this point is written in stone and you may change or replace plants at any time in the design process. The key is to remain loose and open so your creativity can flow freely.

CHAPTER 6

OFF THE DESK AND INTO THE GROUND

Nature always plants in odd numbers.
Wisdom of the Budget Gardener

The most difficult part of creating any garden on a budget is figuring out just how much it will cost. A fast and cheap garden makeover should be approached in an organized, systematic way to accurately estimate the cost of every item. It is virtually impossible to estimate any gardening project without a well-drawn plan, so if you've followed the steps described in earlier chapters you should be well prepared to take that information off your drawing and into the ground.

By this time your plan should display lots of color zones with a plant or plants designated for each. The next step is to finalize your plant choices by assigning each a purchase size and then calculating quantities and cost. Professionals call this part of the process "take-offs" because you take plant quantities off the plan to tally and assign individual costs. In the process, you prepare a plant list and cost estimate sheets.

The plant list may be written right on your plan, prepared on a separate sheet of lined paper, or on a copy of the blank list provided here. It should designate the full name of the plant, an abbreviation for the plant name, the number of plants tallied from the plan, and the purchase size.

AB	QUAN	SIZE	BOTANICAL NAME	COMMON NAME

BLANK PLANT LIST

The cost estimate sheet is used for everything you need to buy, from plants to soil and pots. It's arranged with columns for the item, quantity, unit prices, and totals. This is the bottom-line form on which you estimate all your costs. Fill it in with *pencil* since there may be lots of changes if you need to reduce costs and make the appropriate revisions.

ITEM	QTY.	UNIT	PRICE	SUBTOTAL	TOTAL

BLANK COST ESTIMATE SHEET

PLANT QUANTITIES

Many gardeners go to a tremendous amount of work to create their color plantings and then find them disappointing. The color just doesn't "pop" the way it does in the Disneyland flower displays—the ones located out front where they create Mickey Mouse in carefully arranged masses of pansies. Nine times out of ten the problem in home gardens is simply too few plants. Mickey would look awfully funny if there were patches of bare ground on his cheeks or ears. Disney gardeners pack these beds to their limit for perfect carpets of color, and would all agree that it's better to err on the side of too many plants than too few. This single fact alone is the key to your success.

Now you must tackle the task of figuring out how many individual plants are needed to cover each color zone. To determine the quantities needed to fill the space you must know the diameter of your plant choice at maturity. Each annual and perennial bedding plant profiled in chapter 3 has a designated diameter that you can use for layout and estimating. This diameter indicates the "center to center" of the plantings as well. For example, the pansies in our plant profiles (see chapter 3) are shown as being 8 inches in diameter, a number that also tells you to space your pansies 8 inches apart from center to center for a continuous carpet of blooms. Note that vines and other specialty plants do not have a diameter since they are usually planted alone and sprawl upon vertical surfaces.

Since bedding plants are often very small and planted at tight spacings, the easiest way to determine the quantity you will need is by calculating the number of plants according to the size of the area to be planted. To do so you must figure the square footage of each color zone. You don't have to be too exact about the area, and it's fine to average the dimensions of irregularly shaped zones. But when in doubt, lean toward greater area to eliminate the chance of shorting your planting. Once you have the total square footage of the zone and the diameter of the plant you chose, use the chart provided below to find exactly how many plants you'll need.

SPACING FOR PLANTS BY SQUARE FOOTAGE

Plant size (diameter, inches)	Plants per square foot
6	6
8	2
10	2
12	1
14	less than 1
16	less than 1
18	less than 1
24	less than 1

Pushing the quantities to the high side is also a fail-safe measure in the event you run short unexpectedly. If you've special-ordered a certain color of pansies, for instance, and run out before the area is full, you may have trouble finding the same color locally in the quantity you need to finish up. If you wind up with a few extra plants on hand, keep them in their nursery container for a while as replacements in case you lose a few to transplant shock or poor growth. This is not unusual and professionals always allow a few extras for just such a contingency. Later on you can place them in a flower pot for the patio or plant them elsewhere in the garden.

NUTS AND BOLTS OF ESTIMATING

To simplify estimating, use the step-by-step process that follows to ensure that you accomplish the tasks in a thorough, systematic way. There are two ways to approach the process: Method A, which requires that you draw each plant on the plan, or Method B, detailed above, which requires that you calculate the number of plants based on the square footage of each color zone. If you are working at a scale of $\frac{1}{4}$ inch = 1 foot, then a small 6-inch-diameter plant can be easily drawn with a $\frac{1}{8}$-inch circle. If you are working at a scale of $\frac{1}{8}$ inch = 1 foot, then a 6-inch plant is just too small to draw. In this case, use the square-footage method. Your plan may use both methods, depending on the sizes of plants you intend to use.

Step 1—Make a List of Plants. Whether you are using Method A or B, make a list of all the plants you have shown on the color zones; legal pads are great for this. Later on you can transfer the final quantities to the blank list in this book, or create your own list on a larger sheet of lined paper.

Step 2A—Draw in All Circles for Method A. For each color zone, find the diameter of the plant as designated in its profile in chapter 3. Choose a circle in your template that corresponds to the diameter at the scale of your plan. Using the template and a sharp pencil, fill the entire zone with circles so they just touch one another but do not overlap.

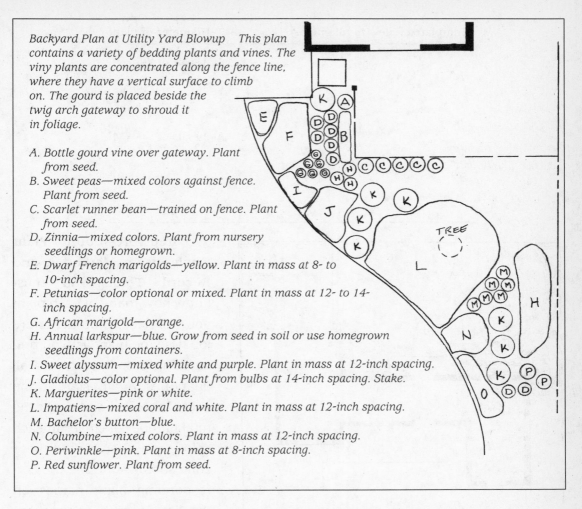

Backyard Plan at Utility Yard Blowup   This plan contains a variety of bedding plants and vines. The viny plants are concentrated along the fence line, where they have a vertical surface to climb on. The gourd is placed beside the twig arch gateway to shroud it in foliage.

A. *Bottle gourd vine over gateway. Plant from seed.*
B. *Sweet peas—mixed colors against fence. Plant from seed.*
C. *Scarlet runner bean—trained on fence. Plant from seed.*
D. *Zinnia—mixed colors. Plant from nursery seedlings or homegrown.*
E. *Dwarf French marigolds—yellow. Plant in mass at 8- to 10-inch spacing.*
F. *Petunias—color optional or mixed. Plant in mass at 12- to 14-inch spacing.*
G. *African marigold—orange.*
H. *Annual larkspur—blue. Grow from seed in soil or use homegrown seedlings from containers.*
I. *Sweet alyssum—mixed white and purple. Plant in mass at 12-inch spacing.*
J. *Gladiolus—color optional. Plant from bulbs at 14-inch spacing. Stake.*
K. *Marguerites—pink or white.*
L. *Impatiens—mixed coral and white. Plant in mass at 12-inch spacing.*
M. *Bachelor's button—blue.*
N. *Columbine—mixed colors. Plant in mass at 12-inch spacing.*
O. *Periwinkle—pink. Plant in mass at 8-inch spacing.*
P. *Red sunflower. Plant from seed.*

Step 2B—Measure the Square Footage of Each Zone for Method B. Use your scale to measure the length and width of each color zone. Multiply them to find the total square footage. If you use a calculator, it's much easier to work with decimals than to calculate using feet and inches. A simple way to convert from feet and inches to decimals is to round off each number, and always *round up* to the nearest .5 of a foot to be sure you get enough plants. For example, 5 feet 3 inches is rounded up to the next half foot, which is 5 feet 6 inches, or 5.5 feet. Jot this number down inside the area next to the plant name abbreviation.

Template circle size (diameter)	Diameter of plant
	At a scale of $1/8'' = 1'$
$1/4''$	$2'$
$3/8''$	$3'$
$1/2''$	$4'$
$5/8''$	$5'$
	At a scale of $1/4'' = 1'$
$1/8''$	$.5'$
$1/4''$	$1'$
$3/8''$	$1.5'$
$1/2''$	$2'$
$5/8''$	$2.5'$

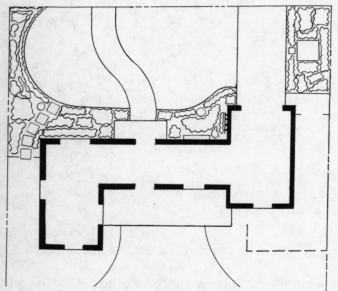

Front Yard Zones   The front yard scheme of our sample house plan is blown up here for greater detail. Calculate the size of each zone if you choose to estimate mathematically, and assign a plant.

Step 3A—Count Plant Circles from Method A and Record Totals. You must know how many of each plant you will need to do the entire job. Use the plant list you prepared in Step 1 to record all quantities. Again, start at one side of the plan and count the total number of circles in each color zone; then record these zone subtotals beside the corresponding plant names on the list. Place a comma between each subtotal to avoid confusion. Once all are counted, add the numbers on the list next to each plant name to find the total number you must buy of that plant. Your final listing may look like this: Purple pansies—12, 20, 6, 33, 7 Total: 78.

Step 3B—Calculate Plant Quantities for Method B and Record Totals. Each of your color zones should contain a number indicating its total square footage plus the abbreviated plant name. Begin by consulting the plant profiles in chapter 3 for the diameter of the designated plant; then consult the Spacing for Plants by Square Footage chart on page 103 to find out how many plants are required per square foot. Multiply this figure by your square footage to find the total number of plants. For example, a color zone that's 15 square feet in size and planted in pansies with an 8-inch diameter requires 2.25 plants per square foot. Multiply 15 times 2.25 to find the total: 33.75 plants. Round this figure up to 34 plants and record the total for this color zone on your plant list beside the appropriate plant name as shown at the end of Step 3A.

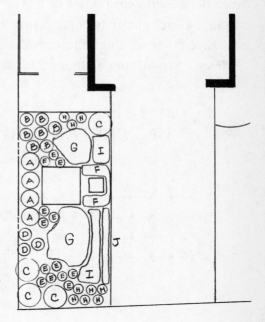

Driveway Plant Blowup   Now our plan has reached the level of detail at which we can actually draw each plant onto the plan. What was once a battered lawn is now a flower garden with a little paved square at the center. Where the plants are too numerous to show every one, there is an empty zone drawn in to indicate where these are to go. To estimate the number of plants required to complete this portion of the design you must count all the circles and estimate the size of each field or zone. Plants corresponding to the letter designation are as follows:

A. Cosmos—pink.
B. Zinnia—mixed colors.
C. Marguerite—white.
D. Hollyhock—mixed.
E. Scarlet sage—red or blue varieties.
F. Sweet alyssum—purple. Plant in mass at 12-inch spacing.
G. Petunia—blue and purple varieties. Plant in mass at 10- to 14-inch spacing.
H. African marigold—orange.
I. Dwarf French marigold—yellow. Plant in mass at 10- to 14-inch spacing.
J. Lobelia—mixed blues. Plant in single or double edging at 10-inch spacing.

Step 4—Fill Out Blank Plant List. At this point you should have listed the name and quantity of plants for each color zone on your plan, whether you calculated by Method A or B or both. Fill in the place on the Blank Plant List for the name of the plant, the abbreviation you used for its name on the plan, and the total quantity. As of yet you have not chosen a purchase size, so leave that column blank.

POTS AND BASKET PLANTS

Just as you estimate the number of plants in the flower beds, you need to do the same for all your pots and baskets. In the previous chapter you learned to show pot and basket locations on your plan, and perhaps you've already created a typical pot or basket to use for estimating. Take a look at the illustrations showing winning container plant combinations in chapter 5 to review how compatible plants are arranged in pots; then use this method to create your standards.

You can break a lot of rules when it comes to plant spacing in containers. For a more densely flowering pot or basket, cut the diameter of the plant in half. For example, 12-inch-diameter plants may be planted 6 inches apart to achieve that lush, explosive color so unique to container gardens.

If you're planning a large party, stick to the very simple program on page 109.

UNDERSTANDING TRIANGULAR SPACING

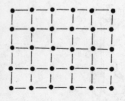
Square spacing

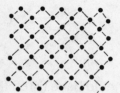
Triangular pattern

When you drive by a well-planted commercial orchard, you can see it is planted in a perfect grid. No matter how you look at these fields they are the same, just like a checkerboard, so the tractor can go up and down in one direction, and then do the same in the opposite direction. If you planted your flower beds in the same way, the grid pattern would be so obvious it could spoil the natural beauty of color displays.

To avoid this, plant in evenly spaced rows aligned *diagonally,* not squarely, to the sides of the bed. When planting on the diagonal, apply another trick: offsetting the individual rows so that those plants in row two fall *between* plants on row one, not directly opposite them. Row three then matches row one, with this alternating pattern carried on throughout the rest of the bed. With this layout, you are assured of very even, accurate spacing of every plant, yet when viewed from virtually any angle, there is no perceived grid.

Step 1. Choose three different-sized pots to work with: a large one at 24 inches wide, a medium one at 18 inches, and a small one at 12 inches. When you design each of these, it becomes a "typical" example to apply to all other pots of its size.

Step 2. For each typical full-sun, 18-inch-diameter pot, choose three different small, upright plants for the center, such as marigolds, red salvia, and zonal geraniums. Then choose three cascading plants for around the edge, perhaps white and purple alyssum or lobelia. This six-plant combination can be applied in all 18-inch pots, but their exact arrangement in the pot can change so they won't be identical. Use the same standard plant selections for pots located in shady areas by choosing from the shade plant list in chapter 5.

Step 3. Choose fewer plants for the smaller 12-inch pots, and more plants for the 24-inch pot, and create a typical design for each of them as well.

Step 4. Total the number of plants for each pot or basket type, then multiply by the number of pots, and you will end up with a fairly accurate estimate of container plants. If you are planning one-of-a-kind pots or baskets, estimate the plant quantities of each separately.

Illustrated Flower Pot Sizes   You will find the greatest variety of pot sizes in the standard red clay pots sold just about everywhere. An entire container garden created with clay pots of different sizes will allow you to gang the pots together, with taller ones in back graduating to the little ones in front.

Tightwad Gardening Tip: Always ask politely if there is a "quantity discount" extended to customers making large orders. Many nurseries don't advertise their flexibility with prices, but commonly will haggle a bit if you buy enough and promise to be a regular customer. If you are a student or belong to a garden club, inquire if there are any discounts extended to them as well. No one expects you to pay absolute retail if you don't have to!

Sizing Plants

Growers usually price plants according to their container size, rather than by type of plant. The larger the container, the older the plant and the higher the price. Sizing the plants you buy by container only governs cost and the amount of time required to reach maturity. They all mature at the same size sooner or later.

In order to complete your planting list column designated as "size," you must decide at what size you plan to purchase each plant. You can manipulate sizing up or down if the cost estimate is more or less than you have budgeted. Let's establish the names of various types of containers used to sell plants before you make any decisions.

A **pony pack** describes the smallest and cheapest six-pack of plants sold, ranging from about $1.00 to $1.50 for each pack. These plants are so young they may not yet have buds. They are popular for planting into the sides of hanging baskets because the root balls are equally small and fit through the holes in the wire. Plants this small need tender care, and if thrust out into very dry or hot conditions, they may wither under the strain or take much too long to bloom.

A **color pack** is a larger six-pack and the plants will be in bud and some will be blooming. You pay around $2.50 for each pack. These can cost as much as twice the price of a pony pack, but you still get six young plants that are well on their way. Larger-sized plants like these are popular for planting into the open top of a hanging basket or pot for instant color, and within just a week or two they really produce.

A **2-, 3-, or 4-inch pot** can run from 50¢ to $2.00 depending on the size. If you buy plants in these single plant units, it will mean a very big difference in cost. But they're tops for instant color, and since they are very close to maturity, they make the ideal choices for short-notice planting.

Larger plants such as mature perennials, shrubs, and trees are sold in containers sized according to *volume* (for example, one or five gallons). It's important to understand how these larger containers work to avoid spending any more than you need to. Since perennials live for more than a single season, those that have grown too large for their four-inch containers ($2.00) need a bigger pot. Growers transplant them to one-gallon containers which are sold for $5.00 or more. Beware of buying any bedding plants in one-gallon containers, as these are not budget buys.

Marguerites and euryops daisies are perennial in mild climates. There, growers offer them only in one-gallon pots or the next size up (five gallons) because they may be up to three years old and thus considered shrubs. A five-gallon plant can run you a whopping $8.00 to $15.00 each or more, depending on the plant and where you shop. That means you pay dearly for size, which isn't so bad in frost-free states since the plants may live and bloom for years. But in cold-winter climates where such plants are strictly one-season annuals, these prices are certainly not appropriate in the budget garden. Just think how many pony packs of bedding plants you could buy for the price of just one five-gallon marguerite!

OTHER PLANTS AND MATERIALS

There are other plants that don't fall into the same categories as the nursery-grown seedlings: those grown from seed, those you plant as bulbs, and those you roll out, as in the case of a sod lawn. In addition, you may need nonplant materials such as mulches, soil improvers, and dozens of other incidentals. Unless you incorporate all of them into your estimate, you may fall short of supplies before your garden makeover is completed.

DOING IT FROM SEED

Growing your plants from seed is the absolute cheapest way to create a garden, but you must consider the hidden costs to know if you're indeed saving money. The combined cost of containers, seed-starting soil, and the seed itself can nearly equal that of a solid pony pack. Therefore, knowing what plants grow quickly and easily from seed sown in garden soil ensures your efforts will be duly rewarded.

Certain plants grow best when seed is planted directly into garden soil, and these promise an enormous garden for pennies. They usually have big seeds, like those of beans and squash, that don't get lost or eaten by birds. They allow you to check on the seed by exposing it in the soil to determine whether or not it has sprouted. Doing this with tiny seeds is nearly impossible unless you really know your plants. The size of these seeds protects them, makes them easy to plant, and helps you keep track of them when thinning and weeding. Better yet, these big-seed plants are usually quick to grow if the soil conditions are warm enough.

The two outstanding warm-season seed performers—sunflowers and bottle gourds—are the secret weapons for shoestring makeovers. Sunflowers are too often taken for granted but make a very bold impact by virtue of their size and potent color. Gourds are summer fare since they grow so rampantly in the heat; they can easily overwhelm a kitchen garden. But screening off a junk pile is as easy as planting gourd seeds around its edges; the vines crisscross into a network of leafy runners in just weeks.

Nasturtiums, sweet peas, scarlet runner beans, and morning glory also have very large seeds that are difficult to lose in the soil. They have a very hard outer coating and benefit from presoaking in warm water for twenty-four hours. They may also have their outsides nicked with a sharp knife to help them get started. Plant these either in containers ahead of time or wait and sow directly into garden soil to save the hassle of pots.

Other plants grow almost as easily from seed and are dubbed "self-sowing" for this quality. Among the best are cosmos, annual larkspur, bachelor's button, California poppy, hollyhock, and sweet alyssum. If left to go to seed at the end of the season, the seed can winter over and sprout the following year just like a wildflower. This quality made them the favorites of gardens planted in the early part of this century.

You are assured a great deal of success if you grow your own plants from seed in containers. But whether you plan to grow plants indoors or to plant them later in the garden, why spend money on special containers? Recycle used plastic soda bottles, which are clear and allow you a good look at the developing root system. Simply cut off the top third, or neck portion of the bottle, then poke holes in the bottom with a piece of coat hanger heated on a stove burner.

Most people fail at seed starting because they use all-purpose potting soil, which contains too much coarse woody material for small seeds and can actually be too rich. You can't use garden soil either since it is too heavy, slow to drain, and rife with diseases that are lethal to seedlings. It's worth the money to buy bagged seed medium, which is composed mostly of finely ground peat moss. It's also sterilized to eliminate any chances of fungus diseases attacking seedlings. Consider how much your time is worth coupled with the cost of fresh seed before you get too parsimonious and cut corners on seed-sprouting soil.

When preparing your estimates, be sure to include the cost of seed, seed-sprouting medium, and any containers you must buy. If you need a coldframe, include its construction materials in the estimate as well, either item by item, or as a lump sum.

BULBS ARE UNIQUE

The one problem with bulbs is that they are strictly seasonal, and though they have a long life span, only a short part of it is in bloom. Bulbs bloom just once a year, and are rather unattractive the rest of the time.

But these are the most flexible plants to work with for special occasions because many can be forced indoors to bloom early, or refrigerated to bloom later than normal. Either way, they can fill every pot you have for a stunning spring party. Summer bulbs are excellent color for summer parties, but aren't well suited to forcing. They grow very well in large containers that are heavy enough to allow staking.

No matter what kind of bulb you use, they are best purchased by mail from large suppliers. Mail-order bulbs are sold in big lots, not like the little net bags holding three or five found at garden centers. You save on packaging by mail and the quality is much better if you stick with reputable growers and pay fair prices. Immature bulbs sold at discount have puny flowers, if they bloom at all, while for just pennies more you can buy top-rated varieties that are fully mature. You may also find the widest variety of color options in mail-order catalogs. Spring bulbs are sold in late summer and fall in most supply houses so you have to think ahead. Summer bulbs are sold in spring.

Since some bulbs, like tulips, are so extensively hybridized, they are available in strains that range from just a few inches tall to nearly three feet. You need to know the size of your variety to determine how many will fit into a pot. Be sure to look up the dimensions included in catalogs before estimating the number of bulbs for your flower beds or containers. Don't forget to include pots, gravel, and potting soil in your cost estimate.

TULIP PLANTING GUIDE

Tulip Planting Guide   *Tulips are the most favored of all bulbs and exhibit variations achieved by special breeding programs. To illustrate just how different they are, the bulbs shown on the left side are designated as species* Tulipa Greigii *and are the same or similar to those first brought into cultivation from the wild. Those on the right are such named varieties as Darwin Hybrids and Parrot and Cottage tulips, and illustrate how breeding has created bigger plants. Certainly the taller varieties are better suited to the garden while those in the middle and to the left are more in scale with containers.*

BULK MATERIALS, SURFACING, AND SOD

If you've got lousy, hard, worn-out soil, the more compost you add the easier your planting job will be. Buy manure or compost by the bag or in bulk and estimate generously for this, because too little soil conditioner may inhibit flower performance. Remember how much nutrition annuals need for their very short but prolific life span.

    Ground bark mulch and sod are to the garden what new linoleum or wall-to-wall carpeting is to a battered old floor. Makeovers, party preparation, or a spruce-up before the house goes on the market are all prime reasons for using these ground cover-ups. Even if you don't replant the bed—even if you don't lay a finger on it—a coating of bark makes it look like a million bucks. This stuff is like saying "I care about my home" even if you aren't a gardener.

If you want to use ground bark or wood chips as a surface mulch around existing trees and shrubs, make sure to keep it from piling up around the trunk. And since it's practically impossible to spread mulch around bedding plants without crunching them with your feet, lay out the bark first and then plant through it.

There is a trick to planting seedlings through mulches. First, get a plastic kitchen trash bag or a paper bag and place it over the mulch next to where you intend to plant. Then, sweeping *away* from the bag, use your hand to clear the bark or mulch from where you want to dig out the planting hole. When you scoop out the dirt, pile it onto the plastic so it doesn't get mixed up with the bark. To fill in around the seedling, simply fold the plastic or paper with the dirt inside, and gently pour the soil back into the hole around the plant. Once the plant is securely in place, spread the bark back around the seedling carefully so its stem isn't damaged in the process.

An effective bark or mulch layer that blocks out weeds and remains in place for groundcover should be at least two inches deep. If you're preparing for a party or sprucing up to put the house on the market, you can use a much thinner layer to save money, as long as it is sufficient to cover the ground thoroughly.

For a shoestring makeover, you can save money by substituting wood chips for bark. Wood chips are a by-product of the tree-care industry and can be obtained for a fraction of the cost of bark, or even free from the right sources. The only difference is that the chips are not as evenly sized and don't exhibit the consistent rich, dark-brown coloring of ground bark.

Calculating quantities of surface materials: You can figure out how much ground bark or wood chips you need in much the same way as you determined plant quantities—using mathematical calculations. You've already figured the square footage of many beds. It's simple to add up all these numbers for a total square footage of the planted area. If there are other places that are not being replanted but will be covered with bark, figure the square footage of each of these as well. When you add it all up you'll have the total area requiring a surface mulch, be it bark, chips, or even gravel.

Tightwad Gardening Tip: In calculating quantities of surface materials required for your garden, use the following conversion table, and remember that area is two-dimensional, volume is three-dimensional.

1 cubic foot	=	1,728 cubic inches
1 cubic yard	=	27 cubic feet
1 square foot	=	144 square inches

When estimating how much surface material you require, however, you not only need to know the area but the volume too. Since our recommended depth of ground bark is two inches, let's use that as an example. Say you have tallied an area of 350 square feet to be covered with bark to a depth of two inches. Since the depth is expressed in inches we must change the area measurement to inches as well. Multiply the area by 144 to express the square feet as square inches, then multiply by 2 (the 2-inch depth) to find the total volume of material needed in cubic inches. Convert this back to cubic feet or cubic yards, depending on how mulch is sold in your area. (Bagged material tends to be sold by the cubic foot, bulk material by the cubic yard.) Calculations for our example look like this:

350 multiplied by 144 = 50,400 square inches

50,400 multiplied by 2 (depth) = 100,800 cubic inches of material

100,800 cubic inches divided by 1,728 = 58.3 cubic feet of material

58.3 cubic feet divided by 27 = 2.16 cubic yards of material

Soil volumes for containers: In order to purchase enough potting soil it is important to know the volume of soil your pots will hold. It is unwise to try and save money by using only natural soil, because even the best dirt will pack down and prevent even saturation of the roots. Potting soil has been specially formulated with enough woody matter to keep it open and well aerated, which is essential for excellent results when fertilizing and watering.

Potting soil is sold by the cubic foot, that is to say, by volume. There are a few simple calculations you should know to accurately figure your own potting soil needs:

Volume of a square or rectangular container = Length × width × height.

Volume of a round container = $R^2 × 3.1416 ×$ height. (R = radius, half the diameter of the pot. If the pot is fluted, then measure the diameter at the midpoint between top and bottom.)

The volume of the pot based upon the formulas above will be in cubic inches. To change the volume to cubic feet, the most common volume used for bagged potting soil, simply divide your total by 1,728. If you are ambitious and want to have material delivered by the truckload, the volume is generally expressed in cubic yards. To figure this, simply divide your total cubic feet by 27 to find the number of cubic yards you'll need:

1,728 cubic inches = 1 cubic foot

27 cubic feet = 1 cubic yard

Instant grass: If you can sew a quilt or piece together a jigsaw puzzle, you can easily install a sod lawn. Sod is lawn grass that has been commercially grown on sod farms. When mature, the grass, including a portion of the roots, is dug up by special machines that turn out long strips of grass about a foot wide with the soil attached. When these strips are laid upon prepared, moistened soil, the roots begin to grow again after just a few days. The strips are laid so close together the seams are no longer visible. Sod is the very best and easiest way to create a new lawn, and can be a lifesaver for garden parties on short notice. The downside is that newly laid sod must be kept very moist, which is fine for the guys at your party, but ladies with even modestly heeled shoes will have a problem moving around with dignity.

The handy foot-wide strips of sod make it easy to estimate how much it will take to redo your own lawn, or to add a new one with a minimum of fuss. Your supplier will tell you how many feet are usually included in a single roll, so you can calculate the square footage for accurate estimating. If you find the process of estimating your sod needs intimidating, the nursery or sod farm may be willing to send someone out to help you. Sod is delivered on wood pallets stacked with rolls. It is wise to add an extra 10 percent to your sod order in case there are any damaged rolls. Be sure to inquire whether there are any delivery fees on top of the cost of sod to avoid any unexpected expenses.

Most local nurseries or sod farms are eager to help you with your new sod project and may loan you tools such as a roller or even a rototiller free of charge. Don't forget to ask for this equipment since the lending policy may not be advertised or the salesperson may simply forget to offer them. Sod grown locally guarantees that the grass type is suited to your immediate climate zone. If there is more than one type of sod grown locally, choose the tall fescue blends since they are more traffic and drought tolerant, with increased disease resistance.

Your overall success will be based on three things: soil preparation, precision placement of each strip of sod, and follow-up care. If you have time, it is wise but not mandatory to use some weed killer on remnants of the old lawn, especially if it contains Bermuda grass or other aggressive running grasses. These runners can grow up through the seams of your sod after a while and ruin the new lawn. Before

Tightwad Gardening Tip: There are two kinds of weed killer sold today. Some are contact killers, which simply kill the foliage of weeds but not the roots. You will see the effects in just one or two days, but soon the plant will put out new growth. Others, such as Roundup, kill the entire plant, roots and all. To do so the herbicide must be taken in and circulated throughout the plant's system, which can take up to two weeks, but once it dies it will not regrow at all. Do be aware of this difference, because a mistake with a contact killer damages plants temporarily, but a mistake with Roundup is irreversible unless it is washed off the plant immediately. Be aware of wind patterns since droplets of weed killer carried by the breeze can affect nearby plants.

buying weed killer, talk with the expert at a local garden center, explain your project, and let him or her recommend a product. Roundup is the most popular weed killer by far, and if properly applied takes about two weeks to kill the old grass completely.

Whether or not you use weed killer, you can't throw down sod on dry compacted clay and expect it to live. Sod roots have been cut and must heal before they venture out into new soil. If you rototill your soil to a fine texture and add compost or composted steer manure and fertilizer *designated for sod,* the sod will reward you with a brief adjustment and rapid lush new growth after just a few days.

Sod is as simple to lay as bricks. Begin at the far end of the lawn just as you would when painting a floor, to ensure you don't walk back and forth over newly laid strips. Be sure there are no gaps between both the edges and ends of adjoining strips, since this can cause brown or yellow lines of dead, dry grass. The strips around the edges of the lawn are most vulnerable to drying, so protect them with a covering of compost to prevent discoloring. Water as directed by your sod supplier or nurseryman for the first two weeks while the sod adjusts, then back off to an ordinary schedule.

USING YOUR ESTIMATE SHEET

All the data you collected while adding plants, bulk materials, containers, garden items, and sod to your plan should be added to the cost estimate sheet. Your estimate will become the master list from which you add or subtract items to fit your budget. You can take a copy of the list to a plant supplier and have them provide you with an item-by-item cost total or just pricing for certain plants. The list shows the supplier exactly what is needed for your entire project.

It will also become a tool in the process of special ordering. Most nurseries, garden centers, and home improvement stores don't stock a really big supply of bedding plants. That's because their shelf life is limited due to their unusually fast growth cycle. Let's face it, no one wants to pay for a rangy, root-bound bedding plant, and retailers hate to absorb these losses. But they love to special order plants from their suppliers, since the plants come in and go right back out again to your yard. If given enough lead time, wholesale growers will even plant the color of pansies you are looking for in the exact quantity you need. Expensive? Probably, but the quality and selection are top notch. Effective and stress free? You bet!

A true tightwad never buys anything without comparing prices. Don't hesitate to go to a number of different retailers with your list and let each one give you their prices and availability. Don't tell them you are comparing prices; some may not cooperate if they know you are shopping around. Most retail garden centers will be able to give you a price for everything including pots, saucers, potting soil, hanging basket stuff, and even ground bark, but you need not buy it all from the same source.

Tightwad Gardening Tip: Professional landscapers know there are always unexpected costs that arise in the process of landscaping a home. To ensure that they do not exceed their estimates, contractors figure an extra 10 percent into their bids to be sure there is a little extra to cover expenses. It's wise that you also include a contingency fund, to eliminate concern over forgotten items.

ITEM	QTY.	UNIT	PRICE	SUBTOTAL	TOTAL
POTTING SOIL	8	C.F.	2.25		18.00
8" FLOWER POT	4	ea	1.19		4.76
FESCUE SOD	500	sf	.35		179.50

PARTIAL COST ESTIMATE

The most difficult thing for anyone attempting a job on a budget is massaging the numbers. The trick is knowing what numbers you can change and which ones you can't. When I design a landscape for clients and the bids come in too high, I have to advise where to shave costs without sacrificing quality. Do not omit plants to cut down on the plant cost because this compromises your carefully organized planting plan. Instead, reduce the sizes of the plants you buy, or grow from seed.

Instant gardens for special occasions don't have a minute to spare. When hunting for cost-cutting opportunities, study your list and see where you can cut a 4-inch pot to a color pack; there is a greater difference in price between these two than between a pony pack and color pack. Can you make the ground bark go further if you use a thinner layer? Can you do without saucers or drip pans on some pots? Will packed decomposed granite or pea gravel work instead of paving units on that little walkway?

BUYING PLANTS

Buying plants is a lot like buying clothes—you may choose from a variety of stores that charge very different prices for what appears to be the very same product. Consider these options for buying plants, illustrated by the analogy of purchasing a new shirt:

Option 1. You can sew the shirt yourself.
Pros: You get exactly what you want.
Cons: It takes time to sew well and may be costly after you buy fabric, a pattern, and perhaps a few notions like matching thread. If you're not a great seamstress the final product might be less than perfect. This is the equivalent of growing your plants from seed.

Option 2. Go to a discount store to find a budget buy.
Pros: Lower than retail prices and no time requirement for sewing.
Cons: Takes time and patience to dig through a lot of clothing to find an acceptable style in your size. The shirt may be a second, and have a flaw. This is like buying your plants from a discount home improvement store.

Option 3. Buy a shirt at a retail shop or department store.
Pros: Fast, always have your size, styles are up to date. Easy in and easy out.
Cons: Expensive, absolute retail pricing, and if it's a designer store you pay for the label too. This is like buying your plants at a full-service garden center.

If you go with option 1, you may pay just pennies for the seed, but beware of the collective cost of the containers, potting soil, and other sundries you may need to get started. If you already have those supplies, then growing your plants from seed is a viable option. However, unless you are a skilled gardener and have a suitable environment and space to grow large quantities of plants, don't give this option a second thought. If you end up with a whole batch of spindly, sick seedlings, all your good intentions and efforts may go down the tubes.

The discount clothing store in option 2 is just like a home improvement store where you get plants at rock-bottom prices, but only during certain seasons. You will sacrifice selection for low cost, since these stores offer a limited number of flower colors; often the bedding plants are grown in mixed colors to appeal more widely to buyers. Like all discount stores, they will lack certain things but have others in good supply. This is a fine place to buy containers as well as other bulk materials such as potting soil, bagged ground bark, and fertilizer at reasonable prices.

The full-service garden center nursery of option 3 allows you to work with the owner or a knowledgeable salesperson to special-order all your flowers in exactly the colors and sizes you want. You pay a premium for service, choice, and fresh plants, but if you have a party planned on short notice, this is the place to get your color packs and 4-inch pots of blooming plants for a weekend transformation.

There are only two areas in which mail order is recommended for buying plants. The first is for bulbs, since these are vastly cheaper by mail and your color range is unlimited. For the artistic gardener attempting a stunning tulip garden, this is indeed the way to get those rare colors that flesh out your subtle palette. Second, mail order has always been the best way to buy seed—both for cost savings and choice of varietal color. If you want ten different colors of pansies, each in its own drift, you'll find them all separately packaged from a seed house. You can also buy seed for unusual plants such as red sunflowers, bottle gourds, or white morning glory vines. For those plants that grow from seed directly in garden soil, this is the way to get plenty of seeds at quantity discounts and to literally pack your beds for pennies.

Before you shop for plants, there are a few things to remember. Be sure you have a way to get plants home, since flats of annuals cannot be stacked one upon another. Never leave plants in your car in the heat as this can cause them to wilt and dry out quickly. If you're making a large order, particularly if it includes pots and heavy bags of potting soil or mulch, the store may have a delivery service you can use. This is particularly true with retail garden centers in the city, and occasionally with home improvement stores. Sometimes they don't advertise the service, but if you buy enough it may be available to you. The ultimate solution is to borrow a truck or rent a little trailer to tow your purchases behind your car.

INSTANT TREES FOR A PRICE

Everyone knows it takes a decade or more to grow a tree . . . or does it? Instant trees have filled every orchard farmer's dreams since the beginning of time, and now, at the end of the twentieth century, the dreams are coming true. Tree farms have begun growing very large trees in wooden boxes, some so massive they can be handled only with a crane. The landscape trade has responded to the demand for these specimens to complement new corporate buildings and model homes. But as with all else in the realm of instant gratification, you pay dearly for these big trees.

Sometimes the need for such a tree is great enough to justify the cost. A $500 shade tree may transform a backyard enough to make a house sell more readily. Or consider how important the shade would be to making a west patio livable during hot afternoons, thus increasing your living space.

CONTAINER SIZES, PRICES, AND WEIGHTS OF SPECIMEN TREES

Size (square box)	Retail Price (+ /−)	Total Weight (pounds)
24-inch box	$ 300	400
36-inch box	$ 800	1,300
48-inch box	$1,700	2,800

Trees do solve these problems, but before you decide on this option you must factor in the hidden costs. First, there is no way you can get one of these babies home in your car, nor could you drag it to the backyard without special equipment. Taking the box off such a massive root system is a struggle all by itself, and then you must get the root ball into the hole, hopefully intact. If you damage the root ball, the tree, your house, or yourself in the process, you risk more than just the purchase price of the tree.

It's not hard to see how important it is to have a professional plant a big tree for you. A licensed contractor will guarantee his or her plant materials. If the tree dies, it must be replaced free of charge. Perhaps even more important is that a licensed contractor in most states must carry liability insurance, which is essential when moving such large, unwieldy, and heavy objects close to the house.

Instant trees are ideal for the special occasion garden, but budget gardeners can't afford to buy such an expensive item just for one party. Fortunately, you may be able to rent them! In fact, you can probably afford to rent all sorts of container shrubs and patio trees for a more complete instant makeover. After all, you only need the plants for a few days around party time, so why buy when the local garden center probably has boxed trees and big container plants already in stock?

If you rent, you may have to pay for delivery and placement of such a monster, but, once it's in place, all you need to do is keep it sufficiently moist. You will have to contend with disguising the box, which can be done with an old matchstick or bamboo blind wrapped around the outside. This natural material really blends in and makes a fine background for smaller pots around the base. If the container is large enough, put small color pots on top of the soil around the tree trunk for even more color, and don't forget to hang strands of twinkle lights in its branches for after-dark festivities.

Not every garden makeover is large, or complicated. Some involve only a little wood deck behind a townhouse, or a simple apartment balcony. On the other hand, for homes in the suburbs with sprawling landscapes, estimating all costs from seeds to sod can be a big job. Don't become overwhelmed, because the systematic approach in these chapters is designed to give any home gardener the tools of a professional landscaper.

One of the characteristics of very successful professionals is the ability to find those experts who have the answers, and to ask the right questions. If you need help, consult a nursery manager, a landscape contractor, or a landscape architect rather than proceed without the proper information. There is justification for hiring one of these experts for a couple of hours to help you with design details and estimating. If you plan to do business with a reputable nursery, their staff is trained to give you all the help you need if you are willing to buy some plants and supplies from them. Above all, know that garden making should be fun and rewarding. Once the hard work is done you may stand amidst your flowers and know that you have stretched every penny of your budget into a landscape that stands out as the brightest spot in the neighborhood.

CHAPTER 7

PREPARATION, PLANTING, AND AFTERCARE

Dig a five-dollar hole for a five-cent plant.
Wisdom of the Budget Gardener

 Now that you have planned, estimated, and purchased the plants and materials for your garden makeover, it's time to pull it all together. This is when your hard work pays off in big changes to your garden, but to assure success you must plant well and nurture the young plants along.

Once you get all your plants home, be sure to place them in the shade where they are protected from intense sun and hot, dry winds. Water them at least once every day, and twice a day in hot or windy weather until they're planted permanently. Not only does the moisture evaporate quickly from six-packs, but the roots of these rapidly growing seedlings are very demanding. Just one hot day can cause a neglected plant to wilt beyond repair. It is also a good idea to give all your plants an extra-heavy watering the morning before you transplant them into the garden.

If the weather is warm, you might want to prepare and cultivate your flower bed soil in the morning while it's still cool; then you can plant in the evening. When a seedling is transplanted in the evening it can sit all night long in the cool, moist darkness to adjust to the new location. Planting in the heat of the day causes stress and lengthens the time required for the seedlings to adjust and resume growing. Keep a few seedlings as extras in case you lose one here and there, which is to be expected.

SUPERTHRIVE: WORLD CHAMPION REVIVER—PLANTER—GROWER

Superthrive comes in a little bottle that looks as though it belongs in the medicine chest. It is not a fertilizer, nor is it a new product. It is an inexpensive concentrate that contains vitamin B_1 and, more important, growth hormones. Plants, like people, have special hormones for different kinds of growth, and the scientists who made this potion packed it with those that stimulate cell division. When you add it to a new plant's first watering, the roots are drenched in hormone that speeds repair of root damage due to transplanting. It's also ideal whenever you transplant anything from roses to shrubs and trees because all plants need to adjust quickly to their new home in order to become established. Put a bottle of Superthrive on your potting bench or in your garden shed and use it every time you plant.

PLANTING YOUR CONTAINERS

Gardening in containers is fun and easy. You can do it in the kitchen or on a balcony, porch, or patio, depending on the size of the pots you plan to use. The most important part is ensuring that your pots provide adequate drainage, particularly if they are made out of plastic.

No matter what kind of container you end up with, you need to line the bottom with a few inches of broken pottery shards or gravel before filling it with soil. This helps moisture move toward the drain hole much more easily and eliminates waterlogged roots. Remember too that a pot that sits right on the paving leaves only a crack for the water to seep out, so place spacers underneath each pot to bring it up a quarter of an inch and free the drain hole.

Don't fill the pot with soil all the way to the top; there should be an inch or two of freeboard space around the rim of the pot. Really big pots may need proportionally more freeboard. Allowing freeboard lets you fill the pot with water to the rim, where it

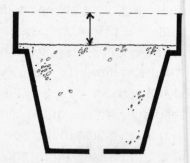

The freeboard space in this drawing, indicated by the arrows, is the recommended size after planting.

can stand while gradually soaking in. It also helps the soil mass become thoroughly moistened, which allows you more time before you have to water again. Little plants will be more eager to root this way. If there's only a little freeboard, you have to water much more frequently and run the risk of dry spots inside or under the root ball.

Little annuals and perennials are tender young things that won't take rough handling. Plus some are more brittle than others. The vast majority of nursery-grown seedlings can be removed easily from their containers, but if they resist, don't be too rough, since this can bruise or even break the stem. Rather than struggle, use scissors to cut the plastic away, leaving the root ball intact. Once the plant is in the ground, be sure you firm the soil around the base of each plant so it sits snugly in its new home. Water well after planting so the root zone is thoroughly saturated.

Planting Hanging Baskets

It's a bit more complicated to plant a basket than a pot because you must first line the wire basket with sphagnum moss, which you buy by the bale. Before you plant, take the bindings apart and fluff up the moss. Soak it in a big bucket of water for an hour or more before you begin.

After soaking, pack the moss around the top of the basket to cover the top wire rim. Do this with larger pieces of moss by squeezing out the water and wrapping each chunk of moss around the wire with its green side facing out. Pack the pieces in tightly so there's no chance of the wire showing later on. Continue all around the basket until the entire rim is coated in moss.

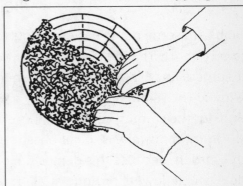

The next step is to line the inside of the basket with layers of moss, allowing them to overlap for a good solid base. It must be dense enough to keep the soil from sifting out the bottom, so when in doubt, use more. When completed, trim off any unruly bits of moss from the outside for a neat, clean appearance.

The only thing that holds soil inside the framework of a hanging basket is the sphagnum moss. If applied too thinly, the soil won't be protected from dehydration, so when in doubt, line it more thickly.

The trick to planting the sides of a basket is to add the soil to the basket in layers. First put an inch or two of soil in the bottom of the moss-lined basket. Then poke your fingers through the first gap in the wires so they emerge at the top of the soil layer. If there's a gap between your fingers and the soil, add more until the gap is gone. Remove your finger and insert the root ball of the first little plant so the roots point to the center of the basket and the base of the stem is flush with the moss. Be gentle with these plants and try to keep their root balls intact for best results.

Continue planting this first layer through every other hole in the wire grid until you've completed the circle. Add another layer of potting soil so it completely covers the roots of the first ring of plants and rises to the level of the third ring of holes. This time, plant through holes between the ones you used in the first layer, so the plants are staggered. Continue adding layers, but leave plenty of room for a ring of plants around the top of the basket and one bigger plant in the center. If you keep adding layers of plants and soil until you reach the row just below the basket rim there will be no root space for plants on top.

Once planted, water your basket well every day for a week or so to be sure the soil is thoroughly moistened and seedlings get off to a healthy start.

FORCING BULBS

Bulbs are some of the easiest plants to grow, but unfortunately their period of bloom is very short. The life cycle of most bulbs follows the same path: the bulb is planted, it sprouts and blooms on stored energy from the previous season, then the flowers wither. The remaining leaves stay green for a while as they work to store enough energy for the coming year, then these too die back and the entire plant goes dormant. A common mistake is to cut back the foliage after the flowers are gone to neaten up the garden, because this denies the bulb vital energy. As a result, the plant may produce small flowers or none at all the following year.

Understanding this cycle is the basis for forcing bulbs—the technique that forces them to bloom at a certain time by manipulating light and heat. Although there are other ways to force bulbs, the method detailed below is one that ensures that your forced bulbs bloom. With this method, they may be planted in the garden for many years of enjoyment. Other methods of forcing bulbs exhaust them to such an extent they must be discarded.

Step 1. Choose a clay or plastic flower pot with drain holes in the bottom.

Step 2. Line the bottom of the pot with gravel or pottery shards, then fill with potting soil to within one inch of the top.

Step 3. Plant each bulb deep enough into the soil so the tip is just visible above the surface.

Step 4. Set the pot outside if you live in a cooler climate, or in the refrigerator if it is a warm climate, but don't let the bulbs freeze.

Step 5. After four to six weeks, move the pot indoors or remove it from refrigeration, and expose it to temperatures of 50 degrees or warmer to stimulate growth. You can expect the foliage to sprout first.

Step 6. Watch for a bloom spike to develop. This is a stem bearing the start of the flower bud at its tip. At this point, move the pot into bright sunlight until the bud matures and the flower opens. Now you can move the lovely potted bulb anywhere you wish. Keep in mind that while you can transplant it into the garden, this is not recommended since you may damage roots in so doing.

Step 7. After flowers fade, cut off the bloom spike to prevent seed from forming. Apply fertilizer designated for bulbs, and water regularly. This aftercare helps bulbs store enough energy to bloom again next year.

Step 8. When the leaves turn brown on their own you can stop watering; the life cycle is finished. Now you must store the bulbs until the proper planting time in your climate. Store your bulbs in a cool, dark, and dry place. Some people dig their tulips out of the pot to make them easier to refrigerate, which simulates cold winter temperatures. Other bulbs may be stored right in the pots, then transplanted into the garden in fall or spring.

Planting a Flower Bed

No matter how large, how small, how sunny, or how well shaded your flower beds are, the most essential part of the entire planting process is soil preparation. Think about it—these little plants must get started, mature, and flower for a long time, and it takes lots of nutrition for all that work. If you get lazy and prepare the soil in a shallow layer, the roots will congregate there and ultimately deny the plant sufficient moisture and nutrients. But soil that has been worked to a foot or more in depth will grow robust plants that bloom and bloom and bloom.

Unless you have one of those fancy minirototillers, the best way to start is with a spading fork, particularly if the ground is already moist to a good depth. If not, water the area well about three days before you prepare the soil so it's easier to work up. A spading fork is better than a shovel for this job because it doesn't make such big cemented clods, particularly if you're working clay.

Once the bed is all turned over, add as much compost as you can while it is opened up to a good depth. The more compost or manure you use the better. Go over the bed again with your spading fork to break up the last big clods and help sift the compost deeper down. Then use a hoe or a bow rake to go over the area again and mix it all up into a much finer texture. Keep working the bed with the rake until there are no more big clods and the surface is as level as you can get it. You'll know when it's done because the soil looks soft enough to sleep on.

Beds are always planted from back to front; otherwise you would have to tiptoe through seedlings to put in the last few plants. However, you'll find that each time you step on your nicely prepared soil you leave a big footprint. The solution is to set out pieces of scrap plywood about two feet square like stepping-stones. These will distribute your weight over a larger area for less compaction.

If you're planting spike plants at the back of the bed, be sure to insert the stake as you go so it is firmly anchored in undisturbed soil at the bottom of your planting hole. Once the bed is planted, water it very carefully. This doesn't mean spray the bed until the surface looks wet; this makes seedlings flop over and doesn't achieve the main goal: to collapse all the air pockets around the roots. It's much easier to use a water wand to extend your reach and diffuse water pressure into a gentle flow so soil does not wash out and expose roots.

CARE AND FEEDING

The key to success is in plant care. Believe it or not, one of the most important things to do is inspect the plants daily, particularly if you're working up to a big event. Regular inspection ensures that if plants begin to look sick or show the first signs of bugs, you can treat them promptly.

The life cycle of most annual plants is tied to seed production, because this is the mechanism which signals the end of its life span. If you prevent seed production, then the life span can be prolonged indefinitely. This is particularly true with marigolds because their flowers go to seed so quickly. If a marigold flower is nipped off promptly after it withers, there is nothing left to produce seed. If you nip off all your spent flowers every day, none will go to seed and your plants will continue blooming throughout the growing season. Keeping your flowers nipped is guaranteed to trick most bedding plants into blooming more prolifically over a far longer period of time.

All that repetitive flowering takes energy, and lots of it. Even the most well-prepared soil soon runs out of nutrition, and unless you feed them, the plants gradually slow down blossom production. This is especially true for plants in pots or baskets with an even more limited root zone. For an extraordinarily colorful garden you must feed frequently, thoroughly, and with the right type of fertilizer.

The best way to feed flower beds, pots, and baskets is with a high potency, water soluble fertilizer applied in liquid form. Liquid fertilizers, such as Miracle-Gro, are much better than dry granules that must be cultivated into the soil in order to begin the gradual process of dissolving. Achieving this in a densely planted bed of small seedlings without hurting them is difficult, and if there's a layer of decorative bark in place, it's impossible. Liquid products for flowers make feeding as easy as hand watering, eliminates burning, and there's no need to disturb the soil.

Miracle-Gro manufactures an applicator gun that automatically proportions their product into the flow from your garden hose. Otherwise, you must mix the fertilizer in buckets, which is both time-consuming and difficult to apply on a larger scale. There are other brands of liquid fertilizers that may do the same job, but only if their nutrient content is balanced for flowering plants.

The goal is to keep a constant nutrient level in the potting soil rather than a series of peaks and valleys. Fertilizer should be added on a regular schedule whether the plants seem to need it or not. If you wait until they show signs of malnutrition, it is too late because the damage slows down the blooming process considerably. Regular light feedings are the best way to ensure your makeover remains in top form, and if you are working up to a party, this extra food will push your plants to maturity more quickly. Professionals feed their flower gardens with liquid fertilizer as often as every two weeks during peak summer growing periods, and you should too. Don't scrimp on flower food if you want fantastic garden color.

Watering

Plants that are heavy feeders also need generous amounts of water. Water is vital in moving nutrients into the root zone and actually helps the plants take them up. The effectiveness of your fertilizer application is not washed out with water but enhanced by making nutrients more mobile. It also helps to prevent any burning in case you overdo it.

What most new gardeners fail to do is pay attention to weather, which can have a big effect on just how much water the plant will need. A good way to approach watering is to examine your own moisture needs. When it's really hot, you drink more. In dry winds your lips crack and skin becomes flaky—it needs moisture. When you're cold and wet, you seek out a dry easy chair by the fire.

Heat waves can make summer bedding plants grow like crazy, but to do so they need proportionately more water. Much of a plant's internal moisture simply evaporates through the little pores in the leaves. If the plant cannot replace this quickly enough it wilts. Even if watered well, some plants still have a tough time replacing moisture in extreme heat because their systems just don't work fast enough.

Wind can be more of a problem than heat when it comes to moisture loss. Wind doesn't just cause moisture loss, it literally pulls it out of the leaves at a startling rate. A single afternoon of windy weather can dehydrate plants so quickly that by evening they hang almost lifeless.

Beware of the wind's effect on your hanging baskets. Remember that they have no rigid container wall to block dehydration—just your liner of sphagnum moss. This stuff can be difficult to get wet again once it's really dry, so gardeners keep a big plastic tub around that they can fill with water and dunk the baskets in for quick first aid on very dry or hot days. Sometimes leaving a basket in the water for a few minutes can be a real lifesaver.

Take comfort in knowing that there are two stages in the wilting process. Just because a plant wilts doesn't always mean it's beyond repair. When denied enough moisture plants show it first with temporary wilt, which is just that—temporary. If you give them a deep drink, many plants will perk up again and continue to grow. Others simply drop their leaves, but if regular watering is resumed they promptly grow them back again.

If temporary wilt sets in and is not promptly remedied with a stiff drink, permanent wilt begins. Once this occurs, there has been permanent damage to the plant, and no matter what you do it will not recover. Unless you keep a close eye on the plant during extreme hot, dry, or windy weather, you may not know if it's experiencing temporary or permanent wilt. All you can do is treat each of the dehydrated plants as if it had temporary wilt by saturating the root zone and wetting the entire plant with a fine mist. This wetting reduces the chance of further moisture loss and encourages the plant to take in moisture through the leaf pores. If it's in a pot or basket, water the entire plant from head to toe, dip the basket or pot in a bucket of water, then move it into deep shade and wait with your fingers crossed.

GETTING IT WET ENOUGH

Watering container gardens can be deceiving. Since you don't see much of the soil mass, it can be partially dry and all you notice is that plants simply don't perform. Use the following old houseplant trick for watering your container garden and smaller color pots in the garden: Keep on hand an old garbage can or a big plastic feed bucket you would find at the farm supply store. Fill it with a few inches of water and set in the entire container or pot. Then water as you do normally until the pot no longer drains and pressure is equalized. This prevents the water from draining out the bottom of the pot so quickly by the old route. After fifteen minutes or so the entire contents of the pot should be thoroughly saturated. Remove the pot and place it where it can drain freely to get all the excess water out, then put it back into its saucer or hang it up. You'll notice a marked difference in growth.

To water a hanging basket this way helps to replenish dry, brittle moss. Use a container that is larger than the basket, such as a plastic garbage can. Fill it halfway with water so that when you dunk the basket the water level will rise to within a couple of inches of the rim of the basket without overflowing it. Gently lower the basket into the water, but do not submerge the entire thing. A minute or two is all it takes for the moss to become fully saturated; add more water to the top of the basket if the potting soil still seems dry. Slowly remove the basket from the water and hang it up to drain. You may dunk each of your baskets this way whenever it is hot or windy to prevent wilt or slowing of bloom production.

One of the biggest causes of potted plant death is poor drainage. The first sign of a problem in the making is water left to stand in the saucer for days or even weeks. This interferes with drainage so much you'll find the potting soil becomes black and sour from lack of oxygen. Such conditions will rot the roots right off even the healthiest plant and it is important to remember to pour out drip pans and avoid over-watering.

For the first few weeks after planting, carefully water by hand with a water wand. This lets you get the nozzle down in between plants and really pour it on. If you water heavily and saturate the soil to a much deeper layer, new plants are encouraged to root deeply. This type of rooting allows you to water less frequently later on since deep roots access more soil moisture that is not affected by surface evaporation.

The problem with spray sprinkler systems is that they deliver too much water to the flowers and leaves of little plants, making them heavy enough to flop over. Sprinkler systems operated in daylight hours leave water droplets on the foliage that can cause burning, just like a magnifying glass can burn paper in direct sun. This also can happen to plants growing out of the side and bottom of hanging baskets, because when you water them in full sunlight they get drenched. Most people choose to hand water in the early morning before the sun is high enough to cause burning, or in the evening to allow all night for the droplets to evaporate.

Many new gardeners tend to water irregularly. This often occurs in gardens where everything is covered by a sprinkler system except the container plants. When you remember to water, the soil conditions are wet enough to encourage new roots, but the first dry spell in which you forget to water kills off these sensitive young tips. You take two steps forward and one step back with irregular watering. Strive to water thoroughly and regularly and your plants will repay you with plenty of flowers and rapid growth.

SPRINKLER SYSTEMS

In-ground sprinkler systems can be a problem in flower gardens. These are the traditional spray heads that water in a fan-shaped mist. Most annuals have great big flowers, and if watered overhead by any means—either an existing in-ground system or a nozzle at the end of the garden hose—the water accumulates on the leaves and petals. Pansy flowers flop over in the mud almost immediately. Tall spike flowers get so top-heavy the entire plant may fall over or break off where it is tied to a support stake.

You'll also find that spray can discolor leaves and petals with water spots. In fact, watering overhead in direct sunlight can seriously burn all tender young plants. To reduce the chance of discoloration or burning, set your sprinkler timer to water very early in the morning so there's time for evaporation before sun hits the plants. On the other hand, watering in the evening is also an option, but this can cause mildew fungus on certain plants, such as bedding dahlia, that is fostered by moisture sitting on the leaves all night. If evening works best for you, keep a close eye out for the white powdery symptoms of mildew or puckering of the leaves, then change your watering schedule.

One other problem that comes up with sprinkler systems is that the flowers grow so quickly they often obstruct the spray pattern of a sprinkler head. When a plant grows in front of the sprinkler it can block the spray so that all the plants behind it die of dehydration. It's simple to raise the sprinkler head up by replacing the riser pipe with a taller one as plants grow. You'll find risers ranging from just six inches long to as much as two feet at any sprinkler supply or home improvement store.

To change the riser simply unscrew the old one from the underground T fitting, and screw in the new one. You can add some pipe dope or Teflon tape to seal off leaking at the threaded joints. Some plastic Ts get pretty chewed up after a while, so you may have to change it too if leaking is persistent. For pop-up sprinkler heads, replace the entire head if the feeder line is deep enough, or switch to a rigid riser temporarily.

Turn off the sprinklers in wet weather, but remember to turn them back on again once things dry out. As temperatures warm up in spring and into summer, you must gradually increase the water flow of the entire system. Decrease it proportionally as fall approaches and temperatures, particularly those at night, begin dropping steadily.

USING A DRIP SYSTEM

The hanging color baskets and pots that look so great at retail nurseries receive the most tender care. Early each morning the staff waters every container thoroughly, usually with a watering wand attached to the end of a garden hose. If you're not familiar with them, refer to chapter 2 for more on this essential tool.

Many of us simply don't have the time or the patience to water our container gardens, which is the major cause for many container garden failures. Fortunately, we can take advantage of a drip watering system which anyone can install. In fact, all you need to operate one is an outside faucet and a do-it-yourself drip system kit.

Drip systems are so simple to make you need not have any formal training to do a fine job. These systems are different from normal sprinklers because they operate at very low pressures. This allows you to assemble them out of relatively flimsy materials without glued joints and special tools.

A typical drip system is made up of two types of tube—the feeder line that is about ½ inch in diameter, and the ¼-inch lateral or "spaghetti" tubing that runs to each plant. There must be an emitter at the end of each lateral in order to control the flow of water and keep the overall pressure consistent within the system. A single emitter wets the area directly beneath it to a foot or two in depth, but it does not cover a wide area, making it more difficult to sufficiently irrigate large baskets or wide bowls.

When it is perforated with microscopic holes all along its length, spaghetti tubing is also called soaker line. Soaker line, when used properly, is invaluable for watering troughs, window boxes, hanging baskets, and very wide pots.

Since a drip system operates on very low pressure, a single hose bib can support an entire container garden. You can cut and assemble your system as you go, or sketch it out ahead of time to help you visualize how it will function. Avoid very long runs of spaghetti tubing because it may suffer from lack of pressure at the far end. Use more ½-inch mainline instead to bring water to distant plants and then drop down to ¼-inch spaghetti laterals when piping to the individual pots.

Two very important yet inexpensive accessories will save you a lot of time and trouble down the road. First is a filter which has two nozzles. You screw one nozzle onto the hose faucet, and the other fits into the mainline. The filter will catch any particulate matter in the water supply before it enters the system. This is important because drip emitters and soaker lines have such small holes that a tiny buildup of calcium crystals or salts in the water can clog them up. If this happens you probably won't notice it until the plant it supplies either wilts or dies. So it's important to clean the filter and emitters often to ensure maximum flow rates and pressures.

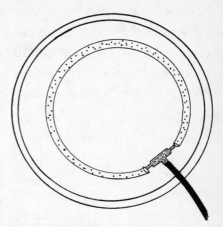

With drip-watering pots that are very wide or hanging baskets that contain lots of plants, do not use an emitter. In this situation, use perforated soaker tubing and a T fitting to create a watering ring that saturates the soil far more evenly. The difference in plant performance is remarkable.

The second accessory is an automatic timer. If you are lucky enough to have an outdoor electric plug near the hose faucet, then you may want to use an electric timer that goes on and off on a prepared schedule. But most people aren't that fortunate and must turn to a manual timer that is spring-loaded like the old-fashioned kitchen timers. You simply turn on the faucet, then turn the timer to the designated watering time, and once watering is completed, the timer will automatically shut off the water. This type of timer was originally designed for drought-stricken communities as a fail-safe method of avoiding garden hose water waste.

You can purchase all these products at most home improvement stores and garden centers. If you haven't created a drip system before it's wise to purchase a starter kit that will contain hoses, emitters, fittings, and detailed instructions. They show how different types of plants are watered and include a catalog of all sorts of other accessories you may need in the future.

The most creative part of drip system installation is hiding the tubing. When you are irrigating hanging baskets, the main feeder line should be hidden up above the hanger in a place where it is least likely to be seen. If the hanging structure is wood, you can buy special brackets that are nailed into the rafter or beam to hold the tubing. If the beam is metal or concrete, glue the tubing onto the metal with a glob of weatherproof silicone. Install a T at the feeder line on top of each hanging basket and run the spaghetti tubing down one of the wires or chains to the basket. Some people like to spiral the tubing around the wire, and if it is a chain, they simply weave the tubing in and out of the links. You might also want to paint the tubing to match your house or awning.

It's simple to add a drip system to your overhead structure to better water your hanging containers.

Top left: *Hide the feeder line on top or behind a beam where it won't be visible, then run the spaghetti tubing down the pot hanger.*
Top right: *You can buy special clamps to hold your feeder line tightly to the wood beam. You simply insert a nail into the little clamp tube and nail it right into the beam. This clamp keeps drip tubing rounded, whereas if you try to bend a nail over the tubing to hold it, the tube will flatten and will later crack.* Bottom: *Solid tubing is shown here by the heavy black line, with the lateral "spaghetti" tubing running along rafters to where the pots will hang.*

For pots that are on the ground, make sure the supply line is never placed where it can be seen or tripped over. Laterals need to be arranged so they come up the back side of the pot where they remain out of sight. If your containers are on wood decking or a porch, simply attach the supply line under the edge with brackets and drill holes through the wood where you need to access a lateral. Whatever solution you find to the watering problem, pay close attention to both safety and visibility.

You probably wonder why some gardeners' efforts are rewarded with more abundant flowers than others'. There is no big secret: those people spend more time in their gardens. While they are watering or simply relaxing amidst the flowers, these gardeners are plucking off spent flowers, yanking out weeds, and studying each plant closely for the first signs of pests and disease. In fact, one of the concepts behind the least toxic method of pest control is to find and take care of a problem as soon as it appears, not after it has become an infestation that is practically impossible to get rid of. Make this your excuse to wander through the garden often, because as you do your eye will become attuned to these little details that make an average landscape into an extraordinary one.

CHAPTER 8

CREATIVE RESTORATION

Repair it . . . don't replace it.
Wisdom of the Budget Gardener

A beautiful garden setting is made up of more than just plants; it includes constructed elements too, collectively known as hardscape. Creative restoration is the process of reviving as much of the hardscape as you can for the lowest price possible. Just as we paint and paper our fixer-upper home to give it new life, so do we cover, clean, and revive the hardscape to give it a second chance. There are many ways to restore things, so you'll find options described here which give you the choice of a fast and cheap or a longer-lasting fix. Either way we remain focused on options that give you the biggest bang for every buck you spend.

GOOD-NEIGHBOR FENCES

In some yards fencing is a very strong visual element, and may be the largest single object in the garden. These are usually six-foot-tall board fences limited to this height by building codes and community ordinances. One of the biggest problems we find in older homes is backyard fencing that has become a mixture of building styles from various neighbors who have replaced their portion of the fence. With this kind of "patchwork fencing" it is even more important to integrate the whole perimeter for better visual continuity.

The first step when revamping a fence is to repair it to the best of your ability. If it's leaning, chances are the posts have rotted out at the bottom. One solution is a simple repair that fixes it for a while by propping up or reinforcing the weak posts with wood or steel. The long-term-repair method requires replacing the rotten post altogether, which may cost you about the same in materials but requires a bit more labor.

Older fences frequently have pet damage at the bottom, and broken or missing boards. Replace boards where they are needed, matching the board dimensions used on the rest of the fence. After such replacement there will be a marked visual difference between the old and new boards, requiring a cover-up treatment with paint or stain to make it all appear the same color.

Your guests will notice your fencing when it is discolored by sprinkler stains, varying colors bleeding through from neighbors' fences, signs of recent repairs, or simply a change in the type of wood in the fencing. You will find a remarkable improvement by staining or painting your old fence a single color that makes every segment blend together.

Exterior paint is the easiest and cheapest way to transform your fence in a snap because it covers everything completely. Paint may be your only choice if the fence has been painted in the past since you can't apply stains over a painted surface. Wood stain soaks into the lumber so it rarely peels no matter how old it is. Paint, on the other hand, is a surface coating which will break down.

Stains designated for exterior use fall into three categories that relate to their relative opaqueness. A **transparent stain** has some color but is muted. These are typically used on new fences as a weatherproof sealer which allows the grain and texture of the wood to show through clearly. A **semitransparent stain** has more color, but still allows a little of the wood grain to remain visible. This is the most noncommittal option since it exhibits both transparency and a noticeable color. **Solid stain** acts more like paint and can do a thorough job in obliterating the wood color while its texture remains. Solid stains have the greatest unifying effect since they have sufficient color to blend new boards with old and obliterate sprinkler stains.

If you were to study a sample pack of exterior solid stains you would find a surprising variety of colors. With so much selection it is curious that many people continually choose the one labeled "redwood," which turns all their exterior surfaces brick red. Such coloring is not only visually offensive, but conflicts dramatically with flowers and plants in the garden setting. Do not think that a redwood stain will make your fir or pine look like redwood. It is better to use softer-colored stains because these can provide a lovely background that enhances, rather than competes with, the landscaping. Do not forget that the fence is a big part of the yard and no matter what color you commit to its surface, there will be lots of it. Your choice of color should also be compatible with your house color as well. A blue Cape Cod–style house with white trim, for example, will blend perfectly with a soft cool gray or whitewash.

The darker your fence color, the more it will show off the "lint" of the garden, such as fluff from cottonwood trees, flowers of mimosa, and spiderwebs. Very dark brown or steel gray also absorbs a lot of heat, which causes the fence to weather more quickly. Dark colors are interesting to work with in the shade because there they can literally disappear in dim light to create the illusion of no fence at all.

Gray is uniquely versatile because it is neutral, and can be either warm or cool in color. Warm gray with a brown base is a standard color and will blend well with earth tones. This is a fine alternative color to a common brown fence. Cool gray has a blue base and works best with white and blue. If you use a warm gray next to a white or blue wall, it will look muddy. On the other hand, if you use cool gray against a beige house it makes the house look muddy.

One of the most versatile and underused colors is green. It may be used with virtually any house color, because green responds to the garden, not the building. A green fence does not provide much background contrast for foliage plants, but this quality also makes it less visible overall. Greens, particularly those that are muted and semitransparent, are soothing to the eye and better for very bright gardens where light fence colors create too much glare. Beware of overly vibrant lime greens.

Be careful if you use a spray gun for painting or staining your fence because you won't have much control of the overspray. Even more important is the fact that the gun forces paint or stain between the boards that will show up on your neighbor's side. This can cause a serious neighbor problem if they have a natural fence or one painted a different color. To be on the safe side, paint all shared fences gently with a roller or brush, and save the sprayer for internal fences and wood screens.

A SIMPLE COLOR TEST

If you're not sure what color is right for your fence or other outdoor wood structures, do what the architects do when choosing a building color. They can't afford to make mistakes on commercial buildings or large homes where colors often appear quite different in bright sunlight than they did in the showroom. Architects test their colors by choosing two or more colors they consider likely candidates; then they buy a very small amount and apply it in separate patches on a sunny south-facing wall of the building. After it's thoroughly dry, they study the effects of sun on the color and make their final choices based on these findings. You can do the exact same thing to virtually any surface you are treating with paint or stain; however, it's best to use a separate plank of the same material for stain testing, as stain cannot be covered up with a second coat like paint can.

WOOD DECKS

Even the best-made decks can become unattractive over time, especially if you've had to replace some of the surfacing boards. The expansion and contraction of the wood can push the nail heads out of place, which is not only unsafe but brutal on bare feet and downright dangerous. Be sure to pound them all back in tightly. If you must replace cracked or rotted boards, try predrilling the holes and using long wood screws next time around. Not only do the wood screws stay in place, they also reduce squeaking.

You can renew the beauty of your deck with stain just as you did the fence. In fact, if you plan to revive the deck and fence too, be sure to consider the visual compatibility of both stain colors. Since the surface of the deck is subjected to foot traffic, it is best stained with a semitransparent stain unless it's already been painted. Go ahead and use a sprayer to apply your semitransparent coloring for a more even, uniform color.

One of the cheapest ways to dress up tired decks and fences is with oil. Wood sealer products in gallon cans are extremely expensive. Fortunately there's an alternative product sold as "deck and shingle oil." The price of this oil is a fraction of that of other wood stains or preservatives, and may be used on everything from fencing to arbors, and, of course, decks. It is quite effective in extending the life of the material, repelling moisture, and unifying the coloring. This oil does not contain any pigment.

You'll find the best prices for this type of oil at local oil product distributors such as Shell or Chevron, which sell it in five-gallon buckets. You simply roll the oil onto the deck surface with a paint roller or spray it on if you have a sprayer rig. Some people like to apply it at the end of the dry season when wood is most dehydrated and capable of absorbing the maximum amount of oil. This time of year is also best because the onset of cold days means you'll be using the deck far less frequently. **Warning: Deck and shingle oil can smell like petroleum after application, but the odor will eventually disappear after a few rainfalls.**

If your deck lacks siding to cover up the posts and pier blocks underneath, finish it off with sheets of composite siding or lattice panels cut to size for a quick fix. Cheaper yet is to plant heavily around the deck in foundation style using big and bushy plants listed in the plant palette chapter.

BUILDING WALL COVER-UPS

Many homes suffer from too many bare, unattractive walls that can be highly reflective and lend that "prison yard" effect. Such is often the case in urban neighborhoods where the surrounding buildings are multistory. Rather than fight the walls, take advantage of them by considering a wall as a blank artist's canvas.

If the wall has a window, treat it as you would the window of an indoor room. Indoors, you might frame that window with a stenciled garland, drape it with curtains, add a houseplant shelf beneath, or arrange favored furniture there. An outside window enjoys the very same opportunities, but here you frame it with a pair of tall columnar plants, drape it with fast-growing vines, or create a lovely flower bed of robust growers just below it. All these treatments create a scene similar to that of a cottage garden painting. When it comes to blank walls, the more plants the better.

If you are handy, consider attaching little ladder trellises to either side of the window and train your plants onto them. These may be made of sticks lashed or screwed together, strips of panel lattice, or a narrow prefabricated trellis if you can afford a store-bought one. Why not build a shelf just below the sill and place a window box overflowing with dripping color and cascading plants on it? Or perhaps line up a row of little terra-cotta pots filled with geraniums on that brightly painted shelf?

Use small-grid lattice panels for screen fences or semitransparent paneling where strength is essential. The big grid panels are better for applying to other existing surfaces, and as such they are often painted for contrast. For example, if you have a beige stucco garage wall, you can apply large-gauge lattice panels in a contrasting color, perhaps dark hunter green. The green grid will tone down the wall, add an in-

ABOUT LATTICE

Lattice has been a part of American gardens for centuries, where it is used in a variety of ways. Its chief application is as a screen to restrict visibility without sacrificing light. Lattice also allows air to move through the screen, which is why it has always been popular for partitions in warm, humid climates. The openings also provide an ideal surface on which to train vines.

Lattice is traditionally manufactured with thin, inch-wide, ¼-inch-thick strips of redwood arranged in a grid pattern of one-inch square holes. In the past the biggest problem with lattice was that these thin wooden strips lost their structural integrity over time. The connections also rusted out and the entire panel disintegrated. That's why we rarely find original Victorian latticework intact today.

To remedy this problem, there are manufactured lattice products you can buy made of plastics. Plastic is more flexible, less likely to crack if you must nail through it, and can be easily cut with garden shears. Unfortunately, plastic does not accept paint well since its surface is too smooth to allow good long-term adhesion, and as is the case with all plastic, it may become overly brittle if exposed to intense, direct sun.

Lattice is traditionally made with diagonal grids, although you also can find them made with square grids as well. You can find larger grids with five- or six-inch square holes. These are not nearly as strong as the smaller grids, but are less expensive since roughly half the material is used in a single panel. For custom applications, carpenters also create lattice that is unique to the job, well-made, and perfectly adapted—for a real custom price.

teresting pattern, and support climbing plants better. If you have a dark wall, do the opposite by attaching light-colored paneling to achieve a similar contrast.

Fake windows: Totally blank walls give you practically nothing to work with. But you can apply the illusion of a window to allow you to indulge in the lovely effects described above. At a junk yard or garage sale, you can purchase an attractive old window with glass. Securely attach it to the wall with large wood screws or molly bolts as a centerpiece which may be flanked by two faux shutters also salvaged from elsewhere. If you paint the back of the window glass black, the wall won't show through. Another option for crafty painters is to paint the back of the panes to suggest curtains or collectibles lined up inside. You can add a window box to this fake window to make it even more effective.

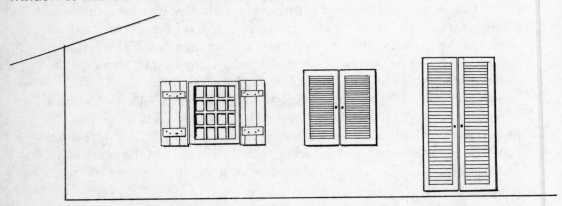

Left: *Here a salvaged multipane window is attached to the building wall flanked by a pair of matched board shutters.* Middle: *If all you have is a pair of shutters, nail them up in a closed position and train your vines and plants to surround them.* Right: *Dream of French doors but can't afford them? Then use a pair of louvered doorway shutters to give the very same effect. Paint or stain as you wish. All three of these ideas may be enhanced by living plants or simply with stenciled garlands painted right on the outside wall using exterior latex paint.*

Mirrors: There's another trick long used by garden designers in the city. Just as we use large mirrors indoors to make a small room look twice as big, the same can be done outside. The human eye can easily be fooled by mirrors, which suggest a view through a windowed wall into other mirror-image garden rooms, or a doorway-sized mirror that invites us to enter another garden beyond the wall. In both cases neither visual dimension exists, yet it lures us in through illusion. The key is to keep the mirror as clean as possible, because any specks or water marks interfere with the effect.

The problem with using mirrors outdoors is that the silvering on the back is easily water-damaged. Mirrors made for outdoor use are not priced for the budget gardener, but for a quick fix, why not use a mirror you'd get rid of anyway? Perhaps you'll find one for pennies at a garage sale or discount store. Look for those already mounted in a sturdy wood or plastic frame, as this simplifies hanging them. At those prices you can afford to replace them later, but in the meantime, enjoy it this summer, or for just this party. Attach it like a window or doorway to a blank wall, arrange your garlands or vines or potted plants around it, and you'll be pleasantly surprised, as will your guests when they discover they've been "had."

Here's an ideal do-it-yourself project for bare walls that will enhance your yard for a party in just hours. Although you should use special exterior mirrors, a short-term fix allows you to apply any kind of mirror that can be attached to a flat surface. You may surround it with lattice as shown here, or something simpler like stenciling or living vines.

Mirrors, like all glass, are breakable. It is critical you hang them securely so that they won't fall down if it becomes wet or windy. A mirror can cause serious personal injury, not to mention the proverbial seven years of bad luck. The best way to attach the mirror is to first generously glue it in place using a paste adhesive designed for linoleum or wall paneling. Then create a strong wood frame that is a couple of inches wider than the mirror on all four sides, hold it against the mirror, and bolt the frame to the surface.

SCREEN IT OFF

In order to solve problems, a few simple projects can make a big difference in the visual quality and usefulness of your yard. These may not be a justifiable quick fix for a simple party, but for a makeover or a big event, these can be useful do-it-yourself projects.

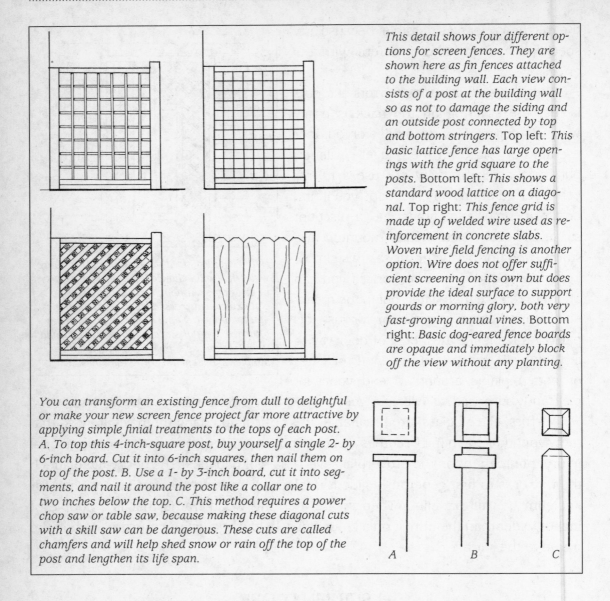

This detail shows four different options for screen fences. They are shown here as fin fences attached to the building wall. Each view consists of a post at the building wall so as not to damage the siding and an outside post connected by top and bottom stringers. Top left: *This basic lattice fence has large openings with the grid square to the posts.* Bottom left: *This shows a standard wood lattice on a diagonal.* Top right: *This fence grid is made up of welded wire used as reinforcement in concrete slabs. Woven wire field fencing is another option. Wire does not offer sufficient screening on its own but does provide the ideal surface to support gourds or morning glory, both very fast-growing annual vines.* Bottom right: *Basic dog-eared fence boards are opaque and immediately block off the view without any planting.*

You can transform an existing fence from dull to delightful or make your new screen fence project far more attractive by applying simple finial treatments to the tops of each post. A. To top this 4-inch-square post, buy yourself a single 2- by 6-inch board. Cut it into 6-inch squares, then nail them on top of the post. B. Use a 1- by 3-inch board, cut it into segments, and nail it around the post like a collar one to two inches below the top. C. This method requires a power chop saw or table saw, because making these diagonal cuts with a skill saw can be dangerous. These cuts are called chamfers and will help shed snow or rain off the top of the post and lengthen its life span.

A   B   C

One of the most vital problem-solving tools is the screen fence. This does not need to enclose anything, but serves the same purpose as partitions do indoors. The problem with many city homes or new houses on exceptionally small lots is that there's no place to store ugly garbage cans, firewood, bikes, and so on. Partitions become the ideal means of separating such a space from the rest of the yard. This concept can also be applied to disguising heating or air conditioning units, well heads, pressure tanks, the base of a large antenna tower, and anything else that is visually unattractive.

Screen fences can be applied in a variety of ways depending on the circumstances. The goal is to build no more fencing than you absolutely need in order to hide something from view. To begin, view the eyesore from indoors through windows, and from other high traffic points in the landscape such as decks and patios where people congregate. The screen you create may be solid or somewhat transparent, as is the case with lattice. Lattice panels are so lightweight they require far less structure to support them than a solid perimeter fence.

There are a number of ways to design screens. A **freestanding** screen rests upon its own posts and stands alone in the landscape. These are simple to build with lattice, and can be created just as you would a single span of fencing with one post at

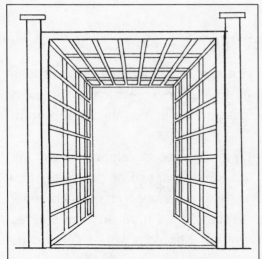

This freestanding fence consists of two posts showing creative finial treatments and a center panel of exterior-grade plywood. You can simply paint the plywood dark green and fix white lattice onto the face for a lovely background for a piece of garden art or beautiful container. Here the illusion of false perspective has been created with nothing more than lattice panels laid out in a creative way.

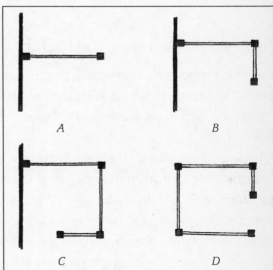

The vast majority of screen fences are designed in one of these layouts shown adjacent to a building. View A is a traditional fin fence with just one side. View B has a second side that blocks the view from another angle as well. View C is three-sided but does not have a gate—just an access opening—and promises even more visual control. View D is a freestanding utility yard fence that may or may not have a gate.

each end. **Fin** fences have one side attached to a building or another structure and jut out at ninety degrees like a fin. These are often very important in tight city gardens where the designer wants to focus the visual in a restricted way. An **enclosure** fence can surround a space on two, three, or all four sides. These need not have a gate but simply an opening for access. Gates are time-consuming and expensive to build, so designing your project so that constructing one isn't necessary will save you money.

A really cheap way to obtain screening if you aren't in a really big hurry is to construct a freestanding screen frame, and use chicken wire instead of lattice to fill in the center. Although it is fully transparent at first, you can cover it in a single season with annual vines. In the meantime, plant longer-living vines in the same place for a future cover-up. This is the same concept used to cloak chain-link fence with a cascading wall of flowering vines.

UNDER YOUR FEET

Paving is a general term for any permanent hard surfacing including asphalt, concrete, and unit pavers. It is much like the carpet in your house, which can make or break the beauty of each room. Paving in the garden can be equally as important, yet too often we overlook it.

One of the most difficult problems is concrete that has developed cracks and water stains. Unfortunately there is no cheap, quick fix except some promising new products which claim to be special stain removers you can use on an old slab. If you decide to apply one of these products to your old slab, buy a small amount and test it in a less visible area before applying it to your patio. Should it work to your satisfaction, then buy enough to do the entire job.

It is possible to paint old slabs, and it looks great for a while. Just how long depends on the quality of the surface and local weather conditions. The problem with this solution is a lot like dying your hair—once you start you must continue forever unless you want to go through that horrible growing-out process. If you decide to paint the concrete for a quick fix, be prepared to repaint it periodically. Some people find the results so satisfying they are more than happy to repaint every other year if that means never having to look at that ugly concrete again. Too often concrete porches of 1920s bungalows were first painted brick red in hopes that it would somehow suggest brick or tile, but this was rarely successful. If you have paving that has already been painted, feel free to change the color if you wish.

When choosing a color to paint your outdoor paving, stick with neutral colors. Shades that are too dark show up every grain of sand or spattering of dirt. Those that are too light show grass stains and black marks from the wheels of your barbecue. Therefore, neutral light brown, warm gray, cool gray, or putty is safest. Don't scrimp on paint either; if it is available, use an oil-base paint, or even marine boat paint that is doubly resistant to moisture and peeling. The better the paint, the longer it lasts.

Another quick-fix trick is to cover up ugly spots on paving with plant containers. This isn't always doable, but when problems occur from rust at the base of posts or columns, or water discoloration along an edge from sprinklers, then this method can work for you. Feel free to use garden art here too, such as cast concrete frogs or rabbits, as long as they aren't too overwhelming and blend with the overall scheme.

Other types of paving which use unit pavers, such as brick or interlocking pavers laid upon a soft sand base, may need some repair. Loose units can be hazardous, as are gaps between units not filled with sand or mortar. Replace any broken units with new ones if you can. To repair soft base depressions you'll need to remove the pavers, fill the low spots with damp sand until level, pack it well, then replace the pavers. It's helpful to mix some dry cement with the sand for a stronger base.

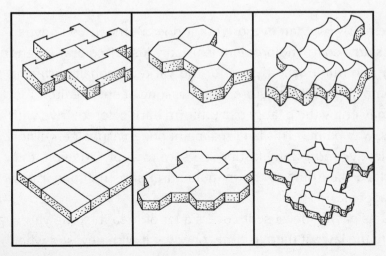

A unit paver may be a brick shape or those made to create interlocking patterns. You may mix and match colors as you wish to create unique effects, but, as shown by these samples of pavers, those that interlock do have irregular edges that must be cut for a clean perimeter. At the bottom left is a brick-type paver that shows how rectangular units can make a clean edge and thus are simpler to lay without a masonry cutting tool.

Most pavers are laid the same way and allow you to build new paving in just a weekend. This series of illustrations shows how to create a level setting bed composed of a mixture of sand and dry mortar. Next, lay out the paving units and tap them securely into place so all are equally level. Finally, brush dry mortar into all the nooks and crannies and water lightly so that all the mortar sets up and binds the paving together.

Aging asphalt can make a driveway an eyesore but it doesn't mean you have to spend big bucks for a new slurry coat. The problem is usually just discoloration and cracking, both of which can be minimized by one of the various asphalt surfacing products you find at the home improvement store. This has long been a Realtor's secret weapon, and you too may enjoy the beauty of a uniform dark-colored drive with a five-gallon bucket of "driveway paint." This isn't real paint but an asphalt emulsion that bonds far more completely, and is long lasting. Be sure to apply an even, thin coat to a dry driveway surface according to the manufacturer's instructions; moisture is the chief enemy of asphalt.

Lawn should be viewed as paving because it covers a lot of area in some yards. You may be able to renovate the lawn if there is time, or cover it with new sod when running up against a deadline. But there are two aspects to consider beyond just the visual quality of the grass.

For a quick fix, go ahead with a thorough renovation of the lawn. Here is a crash course to give you an idea of what's involved.

Step 1. Rent an aerating or thatching machine and run it over the lawn to puncture compacted soil and remove accumulations of dead material. If you have a specialty lawn, check with a garden center expert about the best way to renovate it.

Step 2. Spread a generous layer of fine compost on the lawn and rake it in well to sift down into the puncture holes left by the aerator.

Step 3. Overseed with grasses recommended for turf grass renovation by your local garden center horticulturist. Rake them into the compost.

Step 4. Water generously over the next few days until the seeds sprout and you can see the bright green new blades coming up.

Step 5. After two weeks apply a half dose of turf fertilizer to encourage more growth.

Neat gardens have neat edges. One of the biggest problems can be a lawn edging, particularly if you have Bermuda or other runner grasses threatening to take over. To install edging to an existing lawn, particularly if it's large, can be an expensive proposition. You have the choice of aluminum edging or redwood benderboard, but both are very expensive. Plastic is a possibility but there's no telling how long it will last in your climate. The budget gardener's solution is to buy a straight-bladed spade that cuts a clean vertical line. Although it's time-consuming, a sharp spade can clean up the edges of a ragged lawn just as well as edging materials. For a quick makeover this is the ideal solution and only costs about $20 for the spade.

If your kids and dogs have worn trails in the lawn, forget habit modification! In fact, designers often psychoanalyze family patterns to see where walkways are needed since people always take the shortest distance between two points. Don't fight it; add stepping-stones to the lawn along the entire length of the trail. Dig out the space for each stone so that its surface is flush with that of the surrounding soil. This ensures that you can mow right over the top and need not edge the stones since a collar of grass looks that much more natural. Consider slate, precast steppers, or shards of broken concrete slabs if you're on a tight budget.

There's a new product on the market that really does work well and should be available in most large home improvement stores. It's a rubber form panel for casting concrete, manufactured to give the illusion of brick or stone. The stone pattern is more realistic since it works with the natural color of concrete, while brick would require you to add a red tint. You simply place the form on the ground and pour quick-drying concrete into the cells. If you use Quickcrete, it will set in less than ten minutes. Then you lift off the form and *voilà*—a two-foot-square section of cobblestone paving. The beauty of these forms is that you can arrange them into a walkway, patio, or simply a base upon which to place a birdbath. You can create a beautiful section of paving in a single weekend with nothing more than a shovel and wheelbarrow for mixing the Quickcrete and a trowel for smoothing the top of each cell.

OUTDOOR LIGHTING

Twenty years ago, landscape lighting was only affordable to wealthier homeowners since it was very expensive to install. Today's low-voltage (12-volt) lighting systems sold at home improvement stores are a prime tool of budget gardeners because they are so affordable. You can install a set of lights in just a few hours, transforming your landscape into an evening wonderland. All you need is an exterior plug or outlet, a starter set of lights, and a screwdriver.

Before you buy a set, it's important that you understand how lighting functions in the landscape. This tells you what kind of fixtures to choose and where to place them for best results. The only drawback to low-voltage lighting is that it does not illuminate a very large area, and large projects may require more fixtures than you might expect.

Safety lighting: One of the greatest benefits of night lighting is that you can walk all around the garden after dark without the fear of tripping. If you have a long entry walk or one consisting of many uneven steps, lighting is essential to your safety and that of your guests. These lights must shine on the walkway or path, and are best located at steps, not between them. The fixtures used to achieve this safety

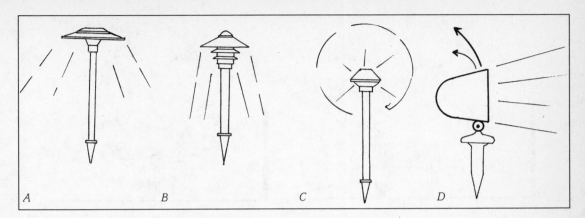

Use different light fixtures to achieve the right kind of illumination.
Safety Lighting: A. This "mushroom" light shines downward over a wide area, making it ideal for walkways and steps. B. Another mushroom that's louvered and thus shines downward over a very small area is ideal for woodland paths where you want illumination only on the path, or along the edges of a driveway. C. Beware of this fixture because it will glow like a weak but naked light bulb. Not strong enough to cast considerable light, it is best suited to driveways or for identification of entry gates. Ambient Lighting: D. This bullet light is ideal for ambient lighting and up-lighting. It sits at ground level and may be tilted upon the pivot point to shine upward at different angles. Avoid using the colored lenses that come with these light sets.

effect are those shaped like a mushroom, with a stem and a broad round cap. Safety lighting is also popular along the edges of a driveway to keep motorists from running over sprinkler heads and lawn. Safety lighting helps to point out the entry to your home if it's obscured by plants and trees.

Ambient landscape lighting: Unless you're into the Las Vegas effect, landscape lighting should appear natural and *without colored lenses*. The word ambient means coming from everywhere without a discernible source. The fixtures are hidden in the planting and arranged to highlight points of interest and lend a three-dimensional quality to a night garden. Fixtures used for ambient lighting are loosely termed "bullets" since they are shaped like a typical floodlight. Adjustable bullets allow you to aim the light exactly where you want it in order to achieve just the right effect.

Bullets are used in a variety of ways for dramatic effect. Up-lighting means the light is on the ground and shines upward into a tree to highlight its branching structure and foliage. For down-lighting, install the bullet up in the tree branches so it

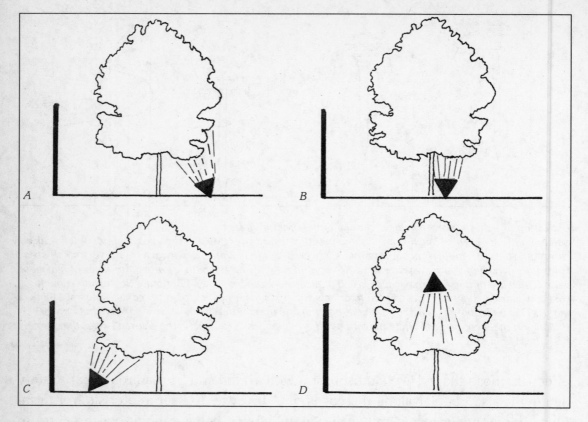

These are four ways to position bullet landscape lighting fixtures. In this case the subject is the tree, and the fence establishes which side is considered the front of the subject. A. front-lighting B. up-lighting C. back-lighting D. down-lighting.

shines downward to illuminate the trunk and areas around its base. Front- and back-lighting requires that you first choose the subject you wish to light, be it a plant or sculpture, fence, or gateway; then, for front-lighting, you put the bullet in front of the subject you wish to light, which is how most billboards are illuminated. Back-lighting requires that you set the light behind the subject, which makes the subject visible only in silhouette. Landscapers use back-lighting to make the gnarled branches of a specimen tree the focus of a nighttime planting scheme.

Installation: Low-voltage lighting is installed after a new landscape is completed, and may be added to an existing landscape anytime. A kit containing the fixtures, wire, and a transformer can be purchased for less than $40. You can also buy an automatic timer that turns your lights on and off at preset times, or a photo cell that turns on at nightfall. Be sure to check whether the kit includes mushroom or bullet lights before you buy. Follow the manufacturer's installation instructions on the kit and avoid installing them in wet weather.

The beauty of bullet lights in low-voltage systems is that each is mounted upon a stake which is inserted into the soil to anchor the fixture. You can both move the stake as you wish to get the light in the right position, and pivot the bullet so the angle can change as well. There are also special brackets in the set to help you attach bullet lights to limbs for down-lighting.

You can expect an adjustment period after you first install the lights. You won't be able to tell if they are aimed properly during the daytime. Sit outside and study your arrangement; consider back-lighting this and up-lighting that to achieve a three-dimensional environment. One thing that happens as darkness falls is a reduction in our depth perception, which makes spaces seem much smaller. But if you light the far ends of your yard the entire site will seem larger. Go ahead and combine safety lighting with ambient lighting to achieve a complete nighttime landscape.

CHAPTER 9

PARTY TRICKS

*The beauty of your garden
is limited only by the scope
of your imagination.*
Wisdom of the Budget Gardener

 The landscape and floral trades use a mixed bag of tricks to create an array of special effects which are especially useful when you are renovating your garden space for a party or event. To really see these techniques in action, visit one of the home improvement shows held at fairgrounds or convention centers. They are usually well advertised, and the best ones fall in late winter or early spring when everyone gets ready to garden. At those shows you'll see little temporary gardens set up by landscaping companies who create them in just a week or two by artistically arranging container plants.

When you attend the show, closely observe exactly how they created the effect. You'll discover that the single most important element that makes these scenarios come alive is water. In most cases it won't be big fancy fountains but little trickles and pools that make a small volume of water go a very long way. Notice too how they use prefabricated garden gateway arches, sculptural lighting fixtures, and unit pavers to create a more integrated space and feel. Some of these ideas are suited to your special-occasion quick fix while others present alternatives to the more expensive ideas you've seen in glossy garden magazines.

FOUNTAINS

Water transforms a patio into an oasis, a backyard into a stunning garden. It is soothing to hear the fall of water that masks other unattractive noises. A lovely fountain used to be exorbitantly expensive because masons and other tradesmen were required to build it permanently into the landscape. Such is not the case anymore since manufacturers began casting fountains out of concrete equipped with little pumps hidden inside that circulate the water. Simply fill the basin or reservoir with the garden hose, plug in the pump, and enjoy the instant effect.

At first most of these fountain designs were rather tacky, with the typical cherubs doing you know what. But today they are sophisticated and adaptable to every garden style both plain and extravagant, depending on your budget. Sizes run from a glorified bird bath to huge commercial units, but remember that the bigger fountains circulate more water and thus generate greater interest and sound.

As long as you're in need of a fountain, why not make it a wise investment in your permanent garden? Choose well by studying the different ornamental features and especially the finishes offered. Don't be satisfied with the plain glaring white; look for the antique finish that mimics bronze, the green patina of tarnished copper, or a mossy green that appears to be century-old stone. Check prices too, because they vary considerably, and feel confident in knowing that the addition of a fountain to your garden is indeed a wise long-term investment. Best of all, if you grow tired of it, simply unplug the pump and move the entire unit out of the way.

A sizable unit can run $200 or more. They are so portable, many party rental companies now include fountains as part of their inventory since garden parties are becoming more popular. Consider renting your fountain when planning an event and apply the savings to more luxurious planting.

GREENS AND GREENERY

There is no better way to enhance a garden than by adding greenery. The soft foliage hides what you don't want your guests to see and provides the ideal background for the snappier focal points you've created. There are a variety of ways to obtain greens on the cheap—some permanent, some temporary.

The cheapest way is to use cut greens, which doesn't mean little vases of boughs, but huge sprays and entire branches the size of a small tree. Remember, it is only for one day, so go ahead and break all the rules. If you live in a warm climate, some of the best greens come from feather-fronded date palms, or from the more beautiful Canary Island palm so common in modern landscapes and as street trees. These types bear fronds up to ten feet or more in length and are shaped just like a giant feather. A bundle of these arranged in a sizable urn can be spread out into a giant fan shape that's an ideal background for a wet bar, wedding ceremony, or speaker's dais. You'll find that a collection of big pots or urns bursting with fresh green cuttings can transform an average patio into a sultan's oasis.

If you live in a cooler climate, consider filling an urn with willow, since it grows profusely in drainage ditches and canals. Willow produces very long, flexible wands that are so straight they are used to make twig furniture. You can use virtually any kind of tree or shrub that produces similar wands of foliage for this application depending on what you can obtain cheaply—preferably free.

One of the big problems with using large boughs in containers is that the weight of the cutting either pulls the pot over or makes it too unstable for comfort. The solution is to weight down the inside of the container. The easiest material to use is gravel because it is cheap and widely available. Place the boughs in the pot and then pour in the gravel. It will not only provide weight, but will anchor the blunt ends of the boughs as well. Since you will want to keep the greenery moist, you will have to plug any drain holes in the container with an old candle stub or wine cork. Then you may add water, which will filter down through the gravel and provide even moisture.

Buying lots of big clay pots for their stability and weight is not the answer for budget gardeners. The best way to solve the problem is to purchase low-cost plastic, tin, clay, or fiberglass pots that are attractive and in scale with the plant material. You may use plastic faux-terra-cotta planters as described in chapter 4. You can use other types of decorative pots as well, even if they won't hold water. Consider a cachepot, which hides the less attractive can or jar containing the water. Check your local restaurants or delis, which often discard large cans that are ideal for the inside of a decorative cachepot. These large cans are perfect for very long willow cuttings or palm fronds.

Another way to obtain real plant materials for greenery is to rent them from your local garden center. Most nurseries keep a good supply of trees, shrubs, and exotics that can be borrowed for a party and returned the next day. In fact, you might check the Yellow Pages for companies that rent houseplants to office buildings, although they may be a bit pricy. Rather than buying a cachepot to disguise the ugly black nursery container, simply use discount mill end upholstery fabrics and drape them gracefully around the pots.

If you can't arrange the real thing, don't hesitate to rent fake silk plants from the party supply store, because if they're artfully arranged among real plants, no one will know the difference. These are perfect for disguising ugly corners, the undersides of tables, or as last-minute solutions to unexpected problems.

TWINKLE LIGHTS

In chapter 8 we covered the basics of low-voltage garden lighting. But the fun comes when you get to use strands of twinkle lights that glitter like a thousand fireflies in the darkness. For the greatest effect, use only clear lights with no color unless you're working with a Christmas theme. When strung up into tree canopies, these lights have a remarkable ability to illuminate large areas and add a very festive character to tired plantings. Run them into your vines and garlands for even more visual excitement. Don't feel as though you are buying the lights just for this party, because there are dozens of ways they can be used in the landscape afterward.

Why not string twinkle lights around the edges of your outdoor umbrellas? Some people simply wad up the entire strand and position it high on the inside of a market umbrella to illuminate the spaces beneath it. Since you are using the lights for a party, they won't be permanent fixtures and you can break all the rules. Run lights along the edges of walkways, on the top of shade arbors, at the riser of each step on your deck, inside large shrubs, and around topiary to emphasize the shapes. If you're decorating with floral or freshly cut greens, definitely weave lights into them for night lighting or for use in the daytime to lend a unique sparkling quality to shady spots. Just remember that if light strands are used in and around foot traffic areas, either tape them to the ground or anchor the wire so no one trips on the cord.

FAKE FLOWERS

There is no way you can make a tree or shrub bloom out of season, but that shouldn't stop you from faking it! Most of your guests probably can't tell a silk flower from a real one except at very close range, but beware of using this idea at garden club functions. The key to success is not spending a fortune on the flowers, which are becoming quite pricy these days. Although it takes more planning, keep a sharp eye out for special sales at crafts stores and floral supply houses to pick up hordes of blossoms at budget rates. If you know someone in the interior decorating trade, ask if they know a wholesale supplier of silk flowers where you may buy them at rock-bottom prices.

When you're ready to decorate your tree or shrub, be sure you do it naturally. Shrubs tend to have a lot of blossoms in the middle and top of their foliage, so distribute your fakes in the same way. You may not be able to reach too high on trees though, so try not to create a ribbon of flowers around the bottom edge. Feather them out as you get higher so they disappear much more subtly.

GARLANDS AND WREATHS

The Romans were great lovers of garlands, and during their holidays each home and temple was cloaked in garlands of foliage and flowers. We too may take the same approach since garlands are so versatile. They may be draped over doorways and windows, snake up posts and columns, and trail down from tree canopies in graceful tresses. You may create garlands out of fresh materials, dried or silk flowers and foliage, or a mixture of both. If done creatively your garlands will blend into the living landscape in a single seamless garden of foliage and flowers.

It's fine to buy finished wreaths and garlands if you don't have the time or talent to make your own. If you know someone who works in the floral or interior decorating field, they may be able to help. These professionals buy their materials and finished products—be they fresh, dried, plastic, or silk—from wholesale flower and plant distributors. They may be able to introduce you to a good low-cost supplier who sells at discount retail, or perhaps they will make your purchases for you wholesale and add only a slight markup on the price.

Another option is to ask around at local crafts stores that sell the raw materials for wreaths and garlands. There are lots of very talented people who work out of their homes, creating dried and silk floral displays at rock-bottom prices. These industrious artisans have little to no overhead and pass the savings on to you. The crafts store staff should know just who is doing this work and will help you make the connection.

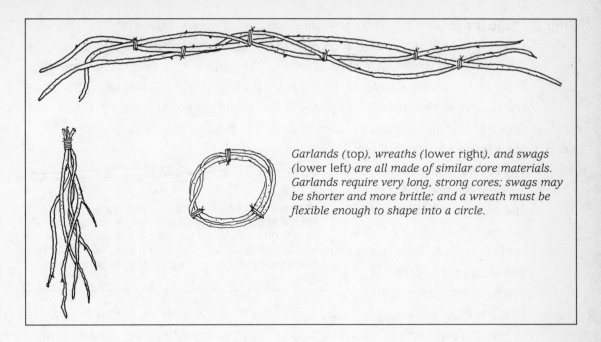

Garlands (top), *wreaths* (lower right), *and swags* (lower left) *are all made of similar core materials. Garlands require very long, strong cores; swags may be shorter and more brittle; and a wreath must be flexible enough to shape into a circle.*

It's simple to make garlands and wreaths yourself, but it takes more imagination to create them cheaply. The key is working with what you have and buy only what is needed. Even if you have never attempted such a project before, there's no reason why you can't be successful at it. Garlands are composed of a long runner or core material upon which the foliage and flowers are attached. The following steps are basic, and you may elaborate upon them or make changes that suit your skills and budget. The basic tools you need are: garden clippers, scissors, needlenosed pliers, hot-glue gun, and florist's wire.

Step 1. Choose your core material: The core material must be strong enough to bear the weight of decorations, and should be sufficiently flexible to drape. You can use material that is green as long as it is strong enough and you remove all the leaves. Whips cut from weeping-willow trees are ideal, as are those of any vinelike plant. You can also use dry material such as grapevine runners. Be sure to cut a good supply so you won't have to go back for more.

Step 2. Adjust the length: You may not have core material long enough for a very large garland. To make a core longer you must splice shorter pieces together using wire. Place the runners end-to-end with a few inches' overlap. To connect them, wrap the wire tightly around the overlapped part, then twist it with the pliers to increase the tension. Make at least two wire connections at each splice point so that if one breaks, there's a backup.

Step 3. Combine the cores: You will need at least two, and probably no more than five, cores to make a good-sized garland. Lay the cores out on the ground next to one another in an open area, then connect

Creating a garland often requires you to lengthen your core materials by splicing them together. Use strong tie wire for this since the splice may have to bear weight or a sharp bend after the garland is hung up. Although splices aren't attractive, you can hide the wire with decorations.

the cores at various points by wrapping them with wire. You'll be able to cover these up with decorations later on or wrap with raffia, a natural fiber available in many colors from crafts or floral supply stores. You don't need to bundle them up tightly because it is the looseness that makes them more charming when finished.

Step 4. Decorate: To keep your garland affordable, use inexpensive dried, silk, or plastic materials. You can grow "everlastings" in your garden for next to nothing if you plan ahead; these are flowers and other plant materials that dry well and keep their color. Some of the most popular are strawflowers and statice, but sunflower heads, wheat, dried red peppers, and herbs are all fine for garland decorations. Mosses—either sphagnum, Spanish moss, or lichens—are also ideal for this application. No matter what you use, each piece must be separately wired or hot-glued onto the cores.

If the flower or decoration has a stem, place it against and parallel to the core material and wrap them together with wire. Lay the next flower on the newly wired stem to disguise it, then wrap the new stem onto the core farther down. This overlay method ensures that you will have a continuous stream of floral decorations. Use a hot-glue gun to attach items without stems. Glue sticks are cheap, so don't be stingy or your decorations might fall off later. Drop a dollop of glue the size of a quarter onto a core or on top of a wire you'd like to cover up, then immediately press the decoration into it. Be sure to cut off any stringy residue with scissors to clean up the garland after the glue dries.

Step 5. Last-minute stuff: It is hard to find dried greens for your garland. If you're planning for a big event, you can insert fresh greens into the garland as long as they hold up for a day or two. The best materials are those with leaves that are thick since these take much longer to wilt than more succulent foliage. If you're planning a night event, remember to thread twinkle lights into your garlands so that they stand out brightly.

Making a wreath is as simple as making a garland. You simply arrange the cores into a circle and decorate them. Wreaths can also be made out of found twigs, bundled dry grass, or straw and just about anything else that lends itself to that shape. Again, try to grow or gather what you can because buying floral decorations can run up quite a sum at retail prices.

PERSIAN GARDEN CARPETS

We don't usually think about carpets in outdoor spaces, but they are a natural. If you are planning a party and are horrified at your patio, consider using carpets yourself. You don't have to use real wool Persian carpets since these are far too expensive. Instead consider the fine acrylic copies you can buy for a fraction of the price. A six-by-eight-foot carpet sells for under $100, and imagine what effects you could create with just two or three in your outdoor living spaces. Best of all: when the party is over you can either use the carpets indoors or roll them up to store until the next big bash.

GAUZE PANELS

There is a graceful quality to the sheer, gauzy fabrics which are often hung as mosquito netting, window coverings, and room partitions in tropical climates. There, air movement is critical to comfortable living, and when the breeze blows these fabrics ripple in the most elegant way. They also work outdoors as party cover-ups for less-than-ideal views on or beyond the limits of your yard.

If you have access to a mill end or remnant discount fabric supplier, consider buying some large gauze sheets in soft colors to hang at your party. Another option is to buy worn bedsheets from a thrift store or at a garage sale, tie-dye them with rubber bands in pale colors, and hang them from an arbor or a tree for a real evening party pleaser. Or you could string an overhead clothesline or wire across the yard and attach the lightweight sheets to it wherever you wish. For even more ambiance, place inexpensive 12-volt bullet floodlights behind the sheets so they are backlit and glow with luxurious color.

Your garden and your party are only limited by your own imagination. There are many other ways to make an outdoor party environment more attractive and festive, although some are quite expensive. The best place to find ideas both old and new is at your public library, where you may borrow both books and home improvement videos. Consider watching some of the newer home programs on TV that present new decorating trends with dozens of useful and creative ideas. Above all, remember that finding low-cost solutions that look like a million bucks makes throwing a party on a budget a real blast.

SUGGESTED READING

Contemporary Books to Assist Your Shoestring Garden Makeover

Barash, Kathy Wilkinson. *Edible Flowers: From Garden to Palate.* Golden, Colo.: Fulcrum Publishing, 1993.

Absolutely, positively the best book out today on creative use of edible flowers in *nouvelle cuisine*. Beautifully illustrated and a must for aficionados of "pretty food."

Boisset, Caroline. *Vertical Gardening.* New York: Weidenfeld & Nicolson, 1988.

An excellent resource for treating vertical surfaces, particularly in urban gardens where every inch counts.

Gilmer, Maureen. *The Budget Gardener.* New York: Viking Penguin, 1996.

The first budget-gardening book filled with ideas that will stretch each and every penny you spend to its fullest.

Ray, Richard M., ed. *America's Regionalized Garden Book.* Horticultural Associates, 1991.

A good general gardening book that emphasizes climatic zones and makes it easier to know *exactly* what grows best in your immediate area.

Toogood, Alan. *Garden Illusions.* London: Ward Lock Limited, 1988.

Well-photographed color examples of actual gardens where our illusions or ideas, and many others that are more sophisticated and expensive, have been successfully implemented.

INDEX